# Understanding Islam:

*A Beginner's Guide to Navigating the Faith, Culture, and Tradition of the Islamic Faith*

DAVID M. EATON

© Copyright 2024 - All rights reserved. The contents of this book may not be reproduced, duplicated or transmitted without direct written permission from the author. Under no circumstances will any legal responsibility or blame be held against the publisher for any reparation, damages, or monetary loss due to the information herein, either directly or indirectly.

**Legal Notice**: This book is copyright protected. This is only for personal use. You cannot amend, distribute, sell, use, quote or paraphrase any part or the content within this book without the consent of the author.

**Disclaimer Notice**: Please note the information contained within this document is for educational and entertainment purposes only. Every attempt has been made to provide accurate, up to date and reliable complete information. No warranties of any kind are expressed or implied. Readers acknowledge that the author is not engaging in the rendering of legal, financial, medical or professional advice. The content of this book has been derived from various sources. Please consult a licensed professional before attempting any techniques outlined in this book. By reading this document, the reader agrees that under no circumstances is the author responsible for any losses, direct or indirect, which are incurred as a result of the use of information contained within this document, including, but not limited to, errors, omissions, or inaccuracies.

# Table of Contents

Chapter 1: Introduction to Islam .................................................. 1
    The History of Islam.................................................................. 2
    Different Groups in Islam ......................................................... 6
    Key Beliefs & Practices .............................................................. 7

Chapter 2: The Life of Prophet Muhammad ................................ 11
    A Biography of Prophet Muhammad ..................................... 11
    The Teachings & Contributions of Prophet Muhammad ....... 14
    The Importance of Prophet Muhammad's Example in Islam. 16

Chapter 3: The Quran .................................................................. 19

The Holy Book of Islam................................................................. 19
    Structure, Language, & Significance ....................................... 19
    Key Themes & Messages Contained in the Quran ................. 21
    Learning the Quran ................................................................ 24

Chapter 4: The Five Pillars of Islam ............................................. 27
    Shahada .................................................................................. 28
    Salah ....................................................................................... 29
    Zakat ...................................................................................... 31
    Sawn ...................................................................................... 32
    Hajj ........................................................................................ 34

Chapter 5: Beliefs in Islam ........................................................... 37
    Oneness of God ...................................................................... 37
    Prophethood ........................................................................... 39

- Sacred Texts .................................................................................. 41
- Angels ........................................................................................... 42
- Day of Judgment ......................................................................... 44

## Chapter 6: Worship and Rituals in Islam ...................................... 47
- Adhan – Call to Prayer ................................................................ 49
- Wudu ............................................................................................ 50
- Daily Prayer ................................................................................. 51
- Jumu'ah (Friday) .......................................................................... 53
- Islamic Funerals .......................................................................... 54

## Chapter 7: Islamic Law: Shariah ..................................................... 57
- Sources of Islamic Law ............................................................... 60
- Application of Shariah in Everyday Life ................................. 62

## Chapter 8: Islamic Ethics and Morality ......................................... 65
- Foundations of Islamic Ethics ................................................... 65
- The Pursuit of Moral Excellence ............................................... 66
- Justice and Fairness .................................................................... 67
- Virtuous Character and Good Manners .................................. 69
- God-Consciousness and Accountability ................................. 70
- Mercy and Compassion .............................................................. 71
- Modesty and Decency ................................................................ 72
- Family Values and Relationships .............................................. 74
- Social Responsibility and Charity ............................................ 74
- Inclusivity and Promoting Harmony ....................................... 76

## Chapter 9: Family Life in Islam ...................................................... 79
- Marriage, Parenting, and Family Dynamics ........................... 80
- Gender Roles and Responsibilities in Islam ........................... 81
- Respecting Elders ....................................................................... 83

## Chapter 10: Islamic Holidays and Festivals .................................. 85
Ramadan .................................................................................. 85
Eid al-Fitr ................................................................................ 87
Eid al-Adha ............................................................................. 88
Mawlid al-Nabi ....................................................................... 90
Laylat al-Qadr ......................................................................... 91
Ashura .................................................................................... 92

## Chapter 11: Islamic Art, Architecture, and Culture ...................... 95
Characteristics of Islamic Art ................................................. 95
Architectural Marvels ............................................................. 97
Calligraphy & Decorative Motifs ........................................... 97
Notable Examples of Islamic Art & Architecture
Worldwide .............................................................................. 99

## Chapter 12: Islam & Other Religions ........................................... 103
Interfaith Dialogue & Cooperation ...................................... 105
Commonalities & Differences Between Islam
and Other Faiths .................................................................. 106

## Chapter 13: Islam in the Modern World ..................................... 109
Challenges ............................................................................ 109
Opportunities ....................................................................... 110
Islamophobia, Extremism, & Misconceptions .................... 111
Contributions of Muslims to Society & Culture ................. 114

## Chapter 14: Conclusion – Embracing Islam ................................ 117
Further Exploration & Learning .......................................... 118
The Universality & Relevance of Islam in
Today's World ...................................................................... 119

References ................................................................................... 123

Chapter 1

# Introduction to Islam

In a world brimming with diverse cultures and beliefs, it becomes increasingly important to foster an atmosphere of understanding and respect for one another. Islam, one of the world's major religions, boasts a rich history and a vibrant spiritual tradition that has greatly influenced the lives of millions of individuals across the globe.

Before delving into the depths of Islamic teachings, it is crucial to approach this exploration with an open mind, free from prejudgment. Islam, often misunderstood and misinterpreted, deserves a mature understanding that goes beyond stereotypes. By exploring its teachings, history, and practices, we can begin to appreciate the vast contributions of this faith to art, science, and the development of humanity as a whole.

Islam, deriving its name from the Arabic word for "submission," offers a comprehensive worldview that encompasses not only religious aspects but also provides a comprehensive guidance for personal and societal affairs. Its foundation lies in the monotheistic belief in Allah, the one true God who created the universe. This belief is at the core of Islam, shaping its moral values and guiding its followers in their pursuit of a righteous life.

The life and teachings of Prophet Muhammad represent a central aspect of Islam. He is revered as the final messenger and exemplar of divine guidance, whose actions and words are a source of inspiration for millions of Muslims worldwide. His teachings, compiled in the holy book called the Quran, serve as a comprehensive guide for

Muslims in matters of faith, spirituality, morality, personal conduct, and even jurisprudence.

Islam promotes values of compassion, justice, and social responsibility. The concept of Zakat, which entails giving a portion of one's wealth to support the less fortunate, emphasizes caring for the marginalized members of society. The pillar of Hajj, the pilgrimage to the holy city of Mecca, fosters unity and equality among Muslims, regardless of their social status or ethnicity. These principles and practices seek to build harmonious communities rooted in fairness and empathy.

It is important to acknowledge that Islam, like any other world religion, is not devoid of challenges and controversies. However, through fostering dialogue, engaging in meaningful conversations, and promoting mutual respect, we can overcome these barriers and create an environment where diverse perspectives are appreciated and understood.

In the forthcoming chapters, we will delve deeper into the various facets of Islam—its beliefs, practices, rituals, and the wide array of cultural expressions that have emerged from its rich tapestry. Our intention is to provide a comprehensive and insightful overview for readers, enabling them to grasp the essence of Islam and its profound impact on individuals and societies.

## The History of Islam

The history of Islam is rich and captivating, encompassing a span of over 1400 years. Emerging in the early 7th century, Islam has become one of the world's major religions, with its influence extending far and wide. In understanding the history of Islam, it is essential to delve into its origins, growth, and development, while appreciating its cultural and intellectual contributions throughout the centuries.

The birth of Islam can be attributed to the life and teachings of Prophet Muhammad. Born in the city of Mecca in present-day

Saudi Arabia in 570 AD, Muhammad received revelations from God through the angel Gabriel, which formed the basis of Islam. These revelations, recorded in the Quran, became the spiritual guide for Muslims, guiding them in matters of faith, morals, and governance.

Muhammad's early teachings drew a small following among the people of Mecca, but as his message grew in influence, it encountered opposition and resistance from the city's leaders. In 622, facing persecution, Muhammad and his followers migrated to the city of Medina in an event known as the Hijra. This migration marked a crucial turning point in Islamic history, as it signaled the establishment of the first Islamic state, with Muhammad serving as both a spiritual and political leader.

In Medina, Islam flourished, gaining numerous followers, both among the locals and through alliances with surrounding tribes. Muhammad's leadership saw the implementation of a legal and social framework based on the principles laid out in the Quran, ensuring justice, compassion, and equality among Muslims. Through military expeditions, known as jihad, Muhammad sought to defend the nascent Muslim community and expand its influence. These military campaigns were not driven solely by religious motivations but also aimed at safeguarding the rights and liberties of Muslims.

After Muhammad's death in 632 AD, his successors, known as the Caliphs, continued the expansion of the Islamic empire. The Rashidun Caliphs, including Abu Bakr, Umar, Uthman, and Ali, oversaw significant territorial gains, incorporating regions such as Syria, Egypt, Persia, and North Africa into the growing Islamic state. This rapid expansion not only brought vast territories under Islamic rule but also facilitated the spread of Islam across diverse cultures and societies.

As the Islamic empire expanded, it encountered various civilizations, including the Byzantines and Sassanids, whose cultural and intellectual achievements greatly influenced the development of

Islamic civilization. Islamic scholars eagerly absorbed and translated works of ancient Greek philosophers, preserving and expanding upon their intellectual legacy. This intellectual renaissance witnessed significant advancements in various disciplines, particularly in philosophy, mathematics, medicine, and astronomy. Scholars such as Ibn Sina (Avicenna), Al-Farabi, and Ibn Rushd (Averroes) shaped Islamic intellectual thought, contributing to the broader world of knowledge.

Islamic civilization reached its golden age during the Abbasid Caliphate (750-1258 AD), centered in Baghdad. Under the Abbasids, the pursuit of knowledge and the humanities thrived, with libraries, universities, and institutions of higher learning becoming centers of intellectual curiosity and exchange. Scholars from diverse backgrounds, cultures, and faiths, flocked to these institutions, translating works from various languages into Arabic, thereby broadening the intellectual horizons of the Islamic world.

Alongside cultural and intellectual achievements, Islamic art and architecture flourished. The construction of grand mosques, palaces, and mausoleums showcased intricate calligraphy, geometrical designs, and breathtaking ornamentation. These architectural marvels, such as the Great Mosque of Cordoba in Spain, the Alhambra Palace in Granada, and the Dome of the Rock in Jerusalem, reflected the fusion of local traditions and Islamic aesthetics.

**The Crusades**

The Crusades, a series of military campaigns spanning from the 11th to the 13th century, were predominantly associated with the Christian world's attempt to reclaim the Holy Land from Muslim control. However, it is crucial to recognize that the Crusades were not solely driven by religious zeal and ambitions of conquest. Islam played a significant role in shaping and influencing the events surrounding the Crusades, albeit often unacknowledged. This section aims to shed light on the multifaceted nature of the Crusades and highlight the impact of Islam during this tumultuous era.

The Islamic world of the time, united by faith, had its own powerful empires and dynasties, such as the Seljuks and the Ayyubids, which controlled vast territories including the Holy Land. Islam was a vibrant, diverse, and sophisticated civilization, fostering advancements in sciences, arts, and governance. Muslims, like their Christian counterparts, held a deep reverence for Jerusalem, making it a city of profound religious and cultural significance.

As the Crusaders launched their military expeditions, the Muslim world reacted with various strategies and responses. Muslim leaders, most notably scholars and military commanders, rallied their forces to defend their lands while preserving Islamic values. Prominent figures such as Salahuddin (Saladin) emerged, mobilizing Muslim unity and reclaiming lost territories. Islamic principles of justice, compassion, and mercy were often evident in Saladin's conduct, exemplifying the spirit of Islam during a time of conflict.

One often overlooked aspect of the Crusades is the significant cultural and intellectual exchanges between Muslim and Christian societies. The Crusaders, upon arrival in the Middle East, encountered a thriving Islamic civilization that had preserved and expanded upon the knowledge of ancient Greece and Rome. Muslim scientists, scholars, and libraries preserved invaluable works of philosophy, medicine, mathematics, and more. The Crusaders, exposed to these intellectual treasures, carried them back to Europe, thereby sparking the Renaissance and paving the way for future scientific and cultural advancements.

Despite the overarching theme of conflict, the Crusades also witnessed instances of interfaith encounters between Muslims, Christians, and other religious communities. These exchanges, though sometimes fraught with tension, fostered dialogue and the exchange of ideas. Notable figures, such as Ibn al-Khatib, an

Andalusian poet and diplomat, acted as intermediaries, establishing diplomatic channels and negotiations. These interactions helped dispel misconceptions and deepen mutual understanding, even within a time marked by strife.

Throughout history, Islam has been a force that unifies diverse peoples and cultures under a shared set of spiritual and moral values. The spread of Islam to regions beyond the Arabian Peninsula led to the development of distinct Islamic cultures, blending indigenous customs with Islamic principles. The subcontinent of India, for instance, witnessed the formation of a unique Islamic civilization, blending Persian, Arab, and local influences. The same can be said for the Islamic civilizations of West Africa, Southeast Asia, and Central Asia.

## Different Groups in Islam

In Islam, there are different groups that hold varying beliefs and practices. These groups primarily include Sunni and Shia Muslims, both of which hold a deep reverence for the teachings of the Prophet Muhammad and the Quran.

Sunni Islam, the largest and most widespread sect, represents the majority of Muslims worldwide. Sunnis follow the traditions and teachings of the Prophet Muhammad's companions and believe in the collective consensus of the Muslim community. They consider the early caliphs as rightful successors to the Prophet, and their religious authority is often derived from scholars and jurists.

Shia Islam, the second-largest sect, has a distinct perspective on succession after the Prophet Muhammad. Shia Muslims believe that only the Prophet's direct descendants, known as Imams, should lead the Muslim community. The authority of the Imams is seen as divinely ordained, and they are considered infallible interpreters of religious guidance. Shia communities further divide into different branches based on their beliefs and practices.

It's important to note that while there are theological and historical differences between Sunni and Shia Islam, the majority of religious practices and fundamental teachings remain the same. Both groups share a commitment to prayer, charity, fasting during Ramadan, and the pilgrimage to Mecca (Hajj). Muslims of all backgrounds strive to live their lives in accordance with the principles of Islam, such as compassion, justice, and mercy.

It is crucial to approach discussions about the different groups within Islam with respect, understanding, and an open mind. Acknowledging the diversity within the Islamic faith helps foster an atmosphere of unity and promotes peaceful coexistence among Muslims worldwide.

## Key Beliefs & Practices

As we move through the chapters in this book, we will delve deeper into the beliefs and practices associated with Islam. For now, let's offer a brief explanation.

Islam is a monotheistic faith that encompasses a combination of beliefs, practices, and principles that guide the lives of its followers, known as Muslims. With over a billion adherents worldwide, Islam is one of the major religions of the world, shaping the lives of individuals in diverse cultures, regions, and backgrounds.

Above all, Islam emphasizes the belief in the absolute oneness of God, known as Allah. Muslims firmly hold that there is no deity worthy of worship other than Allah, the all-powerful and all-knowing. This belief in Tawhid, the uniqueness of God, forms the foundation of Islamic theology and is central to all aspects of a Muslim's life.

The Quran, the central religious text in Islam, is believed by Muslims to be the literal word of God revealed to the Prophet Muhammad through the Angel Gabriel. Seen as a guide for personal conduct, the Quran covers a wide range of topics, including morality, social justice, and the path to salvation. Muslims approach the Quran with reverence, often reciting its verses in prayer and studying its teachings to seek guidance for their daily lives.

Central to practicing Islam are the Five Pillars, which provide a framework for a devout Muslim's religious obligations:

- **Shahada (faith):** The declaration of faith is the starting point of Islam.

- **Salah (prayer):** Muslims are obligated to perform five daily prayers, known as Salah, at specific times throughout the day.

- **Zakat (charity):** Zakat, meaning "purification," is the practice of giving a portion of wealth to assist those in need.

- **Sawm (fasting during Ramadan):** Fasting during the holy month of Ramadan is considered an obligatory practice for adult Muslims.

- **Hajj (pilgrimage to Mecca):** Hajj is the pilgrimage to the Kaaba in Mecca, Saudi Arabia, which every able-bodied Muslim is expected to undertake at least once in their lifetime.

**The Concept of Jihad**

Contrary to certain misconceptions, Jihad in Islam does not solely refer to armed struggle or violence. Rather, it encompasses a broader notion of striving in the path of Allah. Jihad encompasses various forms, including personal struggle against temptations, seeking knowledge, and promoting social justice. Islam encourages peaceful internal and external struggles for the betterment of oneself and society.

Islam places great emphasis on the importance of moral conduct and ethical behavior. Honesty, integrity, kindness, and justice are deeply valued virtues within Islamic teachings. Muslims believe that adherence to ethical principles is crucial to cultivating a righteous character and maintaining harmonious relationships within society.

Overall, Islam, as a faith, embodies a comprehensive system of belief and practice that permeates every aspect of a Muslim's life. Its core tenets revolve around the oneness of God, the importance of the Quran, the Five Pillars, the concept of Jihad, and the cultivation of moral values. By promoting unity, compassion, and understanding, Islam seeks to establish a society grounded in peaceful coexistence and the betterment of humankind.

In embracing the key beliefs and practices outlined herein, Muslims strive to live a life that is pleasing to Allah and beneficial to both themselves and others.

## Chapter 2

# The Life of Prophet Muhammad

Prophet Muhammad holds immense significance in Islamic history and teachings. His transformative role as the last and final messenger of Allah has shaped the lives of billions of Muslims worldwide. With unmatched wisdom and unwavering devotion, Prophet Muhammad's teachings have provided a comprehensive framework for Muslims to live a righteous and fulfilling life.

Prophet Muhammad is revered as the embodiment of the Quranic teachings. By receiving divine revelation through the angel Gabriel, he served as the link between the Creator and humanity. He faithfully conveyed the message of Islam, which encompasses all aspects of life, including personal conduct, social justice, and spirituality. His exemplary character and actions serve as a model for Muslims to emulate, guiding them toward morality, compassion, and righteousness.

Prophet Muhammad's life story, referred to as the Sunnah, not only elucidates the teachings of Islam but also emphasizes the importance of practicing them in everyday life.

## A Biography of Prophet Muhammad

Prophet Muhammad, the founder of Islam and a spiritual leader of immense significance, was born in the year 570 CE in the city of Mecca, present-day Saudi Arabia. He was a man of extraordinary virtues, wisdom, and profound spiritual insight, whose life and teachings have influenced millions of people around the world.

Despite being an orphan at a young age, Muhammad grew up as a respected member of the Quraysh tribe, known for their trade and hospitality. He possessed a contemplative nature and spent much time reflecting upon the prevalent social issues of his time. Muhammad exhibited impeccable character and integrity, earning him the title of "Al-Ameen" (The Trustworthy) among his people.

At the age of 25, Muhammad married a wealthy widow named Khadijah, who provided him with comfort, support, and unwavering belief in his transformative mission. It was during his 40th year that Muhammad received his first revelation from God through the angel Gabriel, marking the beginning of his divine calling as the last and final prophet of Islam.

Muhammad's mission was to deliver a message of monotheism, emphasizing the worship of one true God, Allah. He faced numerous challenges as he sought to spread this message in a society deeply rooted in polytheism, tribal divisions, and social inequality. Despite enduring persecution, ridicule, and attempts on his life, Muhammad's determination to uphold the principles of justice, equality, and compassion remained unwavering.

As his influence grew, Muhammad inspired people to embrace Islam, emphasizing the importance of faith, prayer, charity, and self-discipline. He preached that all human beings were equal before God, irrespective of their race, ethnicity, or social status. This remarkable message of equality resonated deeply with many, empowering and liberating those who had been marginalized by society.

Muhammad led by example, displaying humility, empathy, and mercy toward all. He taught his followers to seek knowledge, pursue peaceful resolutions, and to treat others with kindness and respect. Muhammad's teachings extended beyond personal conduct and into community affairs, emphasizing the importance of social justice, benevolence, and caring for the less fortunate.

Throughout his life, Muhammad also showed immense compassion towards women, advocating for their rights and challenging the prevalent societal mistreatment of women. He emphasized the significance of their roles as mothers, wives, and daughters, and encouraged their active participation in society.

The Prophet navigated the challenges of establishing a just society by forming alliances, drafting treaties, and engaging in diplomacy. He demonstrated remarkable leadership, fostering unity among his followers and resolving conflicts through peaceful means whenever possible. Muhammad's approach to governance was characterized by consultation and consensus, ensuring that the voices of his community were heard and respected.

In the year 622 CE, facing increasing hostility, Muhammad and his followers migrated from Mecca to Yathrib, which later became known as Medina. This migration, known as the Hijra, marked a turning point for the nascent Muslim community and became the starting point of the Islamic calendar. In Medina, Muhammad established an inclusive and pluralistic society, unifying the local tribes and resolving long-standing disputes.

Throughout his life, Prophet Muhammad faced numerous military conflicts and challenges from various factions. However, he always sought peaceful resolutions and prioritized the preservation of life. His example of mercy and forgiveness even toward his staunchest enemies set a precedent for generations of Muslims, embodying the essence of Islam as a religion of peace.

Muhammad passed away in 632 CE, leaving behind a legacy that shaped the course of human history. His teachings and actions continue to inspire millions of believers around the world, guiding them towards a path of personal growth, social justice, and spiritual enlightenment.

Prophet Muhammad's life remains a testament to the power of compassion, humility, and perseverance. His unwavering commitment to justice and equality serves as a timeless reminder of the core values that bind humanity. Muhammad's biography stands as a remarkable testament to the profound impact an individual can have on the world through a life devoted to noble principles and divine guidance.

## The Teachings & Contributions of Prophet Muhammad

One of the most profound teachings of Prophet Muhammad was his emphasis on monotheism. He revealed to his followers the concept of Tawhid, the belief in the absolute unity and oneness of God. This teaching spoke directly against the prevalent polytheistic beliefs in Arabia, encouraging people to abandon their idols and worship the one true God.

Prophet Muhammad stressed the importance of a personal and direct relationship between individuals and God, free from intermediaries, rituals, or superstitions. This teaching continues to be the cornerstone of Islamic faith, guiding Muslims to this day to recognize the divine presence in all aspects of life.

Muhammad's teachings also emphasized the importance of moral virtues and ethical conduct. He taught his followers to embody qualities such as honesty, compassion, integrity, humility, and justice. Muhammad's teachings upheld the values of social harmony, challenging the prevailing social hierarchies and promoting equality amongst individuals regardless of their race, social status, or gender. He rejected discrimination and violence, promoting love, compassion, and forgiveness as the foundations of a just and peaceful society. His teachings were aimed at creating a community that would prioritize the welfare and well-being of all its members.

Furthermore, Prophet Muhammad made significant contributions to social reforms during his time. As mentioned, he championed women's rights, challenging the patriarchal norms that treated women as property or second-class citizens. Muhammad advocated for the education and empowerment of women, granting them rights to own property, to inherit, and to participate in social and political affairs. His teachings promoted the importance of mutual respect and partnership within marriage, ensuring the fair treatment and welfare of women within society.

Muhammad's teachings also addressed economic inequalities and promoted social welfare. He emphasized the importance of charity, advocating for the redistribution of wealth and resources to alleviate poverty and create a more just society. His exemplification of generosity and compassion inspired many of his followers to actively engage in acts of charity and philanthropy, leading to the establishment of a social welfare system within the early Islamic society.

Prophet Muhammad's contributions extended beyond the spiritual realm. He also played a pivotal role in establishing a comprehensive legal system known as Shariah, which aimed at providing guidance and justice to individuals within a community. This system promoted the rule of law, ensured the protection of human rights, and encouraged the resolving of disputes through fair and objective means. The principles of justice, equity, and impartiality that underpinned Muhammad's legal reforms remain crucial in contemporary Islamic societies.

In addition to these teachings and contributions, Prophet Muhammad's life serves as an inspiration by demonstrating immense resilience in the face of adversity. He faced persecution, exile, and even attempted assassination for his beliefs and teachings. Despite these challenges, he maintained his unwavering commitment to his message of peace, justice, and unity. His leadership and ability to unite diverse communities stand as a testament to his character and vision.

# The Importance of Prophet Muhammad's Example in Islam

Prophet Muhammad is not only revered as the final prophet of Islam but also as a source of guidance and inspiration for believers. His example serves as an essential focal point for Muslims in understanding and practicing the teachings of Islam.

The importance of Prophet Muhammad's example can be seen in various aspects of life, including personal conduct, social interactions, justice, and spirituality. His life was a manifestation of the most noble qualities and virtues, providing an impeccable model for Muslims to follow.

In terms of personal conduct, Prophet Muhammad exemplified the highest moral character. He was known for his honesty, integrity, humility, and kindness. His impeccable honesty earned him the title of "Al-Amin," the trustworthy. Muslims are encouraged to emulate his virtuous character, seeking to be honest in their dealings, kind to others, and modest in their behavior.

Prophet Muhammad's example extends to social interactions as well. We have already explored how he emphasized the importance of unity, respect, and compassion within the community. He promoted equality and justice, treating people fairly regardless of their social status, race, or gender. He was known for his kindness toward orphans, widows, and all those who were marginalized in society. Muslims are therefore encouraged to follow his footsteps by fostering inclusive communities, treating others with respect, and upholding justice for all.

In matters of justice, Prophet Muhammad's example shines through. He established a system of justice that was based on fairness, impartiality, and respect for the rule of law. His emphasis on justice serves as a reminder to Muslims to fight injustice and oppression in all its forms.

Prophet Muhammad's spiritual example is particularly resonate for Muslims as well. His relationship with God was of utmost importance to him and it reflected in every aspect of his life. Muslims strive to follow his example by participating in regular prayer, contemplation, acts of charity, and adhering to the principles of Islam. His spirituality serves as a reminder for Muslims to remain steadfast in their faith and to nurture a deep connection with their Creator.

Furthermore, Prophet Muhammad's example serves as a source of inspiration for Muslims to overcome challenges and difficulties. His life was filled with trials and tribulations, yet he faced them with unwavering faith, patience, and perseverance. His example teaches Muslims to remain steadfast in the face of adversity, to remain hopeful during times of difficulty, and to trust in God's wisdom and guidance.

In essence, the importance of Prophet Muhammad's example in Islam cannot be overstated. His exemplary life serves as a guide for Muslims in navigating their personal, social, and spiritual lives. By emulating his virtues and incorporating his teachings into their daily lives, Muslims aim to seek the pleasure of God, promote goodness, and contribute positively to society.

## Chapter 3

# The Quran

## The Holy Book of Islam

The Quran, also known as the Koran, is the holy book of Islam. It is believed by Muslims to be the word of God as revealed to the Prophet Muhammad through the archangel Gabriel. The Quran serves as a comprehensive guidebook for Muslims, providing them with moral and ethical principles, spiritual guidance, and a blueprint for leading a righteous life.

The Quran is structured in a poetic form, with each chapter containing various verses, or ayahs. These verses are arranged in a manner that emphasizes rhythm, flow, and harmony, adding to the aesthetic appeal of the text. Muslims often recite the Quran during prayers and seek solace and tranquility from its melodic and rhythmic recitation.

### Structure, Language, & Significance

The Quran holds profound religious and literary significance for Muslims worldwide. It has captivated readers for centuries with its eloquence, linguistic beauty, and rich structure.

The Quran is written in Arabic, the revelation language of Islam, and is considered by Muslims to be the literal and exact words of God. As a result, the Quran is revered as the unaltered and direct message from God to humanity. Its poetic nature, known as saj', contributes to the beauty and fluidity of its verses, making it easy to memorize and recite. However, the Quran has also been translated into other languages, creating an inclusive approach to the religion.

One of the most remarkable aspects of the Quranic language is its ability to convey complex concepts in succinct phrases. This brevity, coupled with layered meanings, necessitates deep reflection and contemplation. The text often employs vivid metaphors, allegories, parables, and rhetorical devices to communicate profound spiritual truths. Through its linguistic mastery, the Quran elevates the spiritual experience for believers while welcoming readers from diverse linguistic backgrounds to explore its teachings.

**Structure**

The Quran comprises 114 chapters, known as surahs, varying in length from a few lines to several pages. These surahs are further divided into verses, called ayat, combining to form a cohesive and structured framework. The arrangement of the chapters is not chronological but rather follows a divine organization known only to Allah.

The Quran's structure also incorporates numerical patterns, adding to its intrigue. Some surahs begin with certain letters, known as the Muqatta'at, the meanings of which remain a subject of discussion among scholars. This pattern adds a rhythmic and harmonious quality to its recitation. Moreover, the verses contain an inherent symmetry, marked by pauses and repetition, emphasizing important themes or ideas.

**Significance**

The Quran holds immense significance for Muslims as the direct word of Allah revealed to the Prophet Muhammad over a span of 23 years. It serves as the ultimate guide, encompassing matters of faith, morality, guidance, and legislation. The significance of the Quran is multifaceted, encompassing both its spiritual and practical implications.

Spiritually, the Quran serves as a source of inspiration, solace, and guidance for Muslims. Its verses offer profound insights into the purpose of life, the nature of God, and the principles of righteousness. It fosters a deep connection between believers and the divine, providing a roadmap for navigating life's challenges and fostering personal growth.

The Quran also plays a crucial role in shaping Islamic law—Sharia. It contains a comprehensive ethical framework outlining principles of justice, compassion, and social responsibility. The Quran's verses on legal matters provide guidelines for personal conduct, family matters, commerce, crime, and societal issues, ensuring a just and harmonious societal order. Muslims turn to the Quran to glean these principles and apply them to contemporary contexts.

Furthermore, the Quran's linguistic and structural qualities have inspired artistic expressions, including recitation, calligraphy, and poetry. Its musical recitation, or Tajweed, captivates listeners with its melodious tones, further emphasizing the beauty of its message. The art of Quranic calligraphy represents a fusion of visual artistry and religious devotion, creating intricate designs that evoke a sense of awe and reverence.

## Key Themes & Messages Contained in the Quran

Within its pages, the Quran presents a wide array of themes and messages, offering guidance, wisdom, and inspiration for individuals seeking a righteous path. In this section, let's explore some of the key themes and messages found within the Quran, shedding light on their importance and impact on Muslims' lives.

### Monotheism and Divine Unity

The foremost theme in the Quran is the concept of monotheism or Tawhid, emphasizing the belief in the oneness of God (Allah). The Quran repeatedly reinforces the idea that there is only one God worthy of worship. This central message promotes the unity of humankind, eradicating all forms of idolatry and emphasizing the need for devotion to a singular higher power.

**Guidance and Moral Teachings**

The Quran serves as a guide for Muslims, providing them with moral teachings and ethical guidelines. It asserts the importance of leading a righteous life, promoting virtues such as justice, compassion, honesty, and humility. The Quran encourages Muslims to strive for excellence, to be mindful of their actions, and to treat others with kindness and respect.

**The Day of Judgment**

The Quran extensively addresses the concept of the Day of Judgment, underscoring the belief that each person will be held accountable for their deeds in the hereafter. It emphasizes the importance of leading a righteous life and warns against succumbing to worldly temptations.

The Quran's messages about the Day of Judgment instill a sense of responsibility, inspiring Muslims to seek forgiveness, perform good deeds, and strive for salvation.

**Universal Brotherhood and Social Justice**

Promoting unity and peaceful coexistence, the Quran repeatedly stresses the concept of universal brotherhood among Muslims and all of humanity. It highlights the equality of all individuals, regardless of their race, ethnicity, or social status. The Quran calls for justice and fairness in society, emphasizing the need to help the poor, respect human rights, and alleviate societal inequalities.

**Patience and Perseverance**

One recurring theme in the Quran is the importance of patience and perseverance in the face of hardships and trials. It reminds Muslims that challenges are a part of life, and that through patience, they can overcome difficulties. This message instills in believers the determination to remain steadfast and optimistic, even in the face of adversity.

## Knowledge and Learning

The Quran places great emphasis on seeking knowledge and encourages Muslims to be lifelong learners. It highlights the importance of intellectual growth, critical thinking, and the pursuit of knowledge in various fields. The Quran recognizes knowledge as a means to deepen one's faith, enrich society, and contribute to the betterment of the world.

## Mercy and Forgiveness

Throughout the Quran, the attributes of mercy and forgiveness are repeatedly mentioned in relation to Allah. It emphasizes that Allah is the Most Merciful and encourages Muslims to embody these qualities in their interactions with others. The Quran promotes forgiveness, both seeking and granting it, as a means of spiritual growth and interpersonal harmony.

The Quran encompasses a vast array of themes and messages, providing profound guidance to Muslims across the globe. Through its teachings, it emphasizes the importance of monotheism, providing moral guidance, and fostering universal brotherhood. Additionally, the Quran encourages patience, knowledge, and forgiveness as means to lead a righteous life.

By understanding and implementing these key themes, Muslims strive to cultivate a strong connection with Allah, navigate challenges, and contribute positively to society at large.

## Learning the Quran

Muslims learn about the Quran through a variety of means, as it holds tremendous importance in their spiritual and intellectual lives.

Here are some key ways in which Muslims acquire knowledge of the Quran:

- **Recitation and memorization:** The oral tradition of reciting and memorizing the Quran is deeply ingrained in Muslim culture. From an early age, children receive guidance and education from scholars, teachers, family members, and Quran memorization centers (called madrasas). Through repetition and diligent practice, individuals commit the entire Quran to memory, ensuring that its words are preserved accurately.

- **Quranic Schools and education:** Many Muslim-majority countries have established institutions solely dedicated to teaching the Quran and its interpretation. Students attend Quranic schools (known as madrasas or maktab) alongside their regular educational curriculum. In these schools, they learn Arabic, the language of the Quran, and study various aspects of Islamic learning, including recitation styles, rules of Tajweed (pronunciation and phonetics), and the application of Quranic principles in daily life.

- **Personal study:** Muslims also engage in personal study of the Quran, either independently or with the assistance of scholars and Islamic literature. They read translations of the Quran in their native languages to gain a better understanding of its meanings. Additionally, they delve into the historical context, interpretive exegesis (tafsir), and linguistic nuances to gain deeper insights into the divine message.

- **Tafsir:** Tafsir refers to the scholarly interpretation and commentary on the Quran. Knowledgeable scholars dedicate their lives to studying and explaining the Quran, elucidating its wisdom, and clarifying its teachings. These commentaries address linguistic, historical, cultural, and societal contexts, providing valuable insights to learners to better understand the verses and their significance.

- **Online resources:** With the advancement of technology, Muslims now have access to numerous online resources that facilitate Quranic learning. Websites, mobile applications, and online platforms offer Quranic recitations, translations, commentaries, study guides, and interactive courses, making it convenient for individuals to access Quranic knowledge from anywhere in the world.

Overall, Muslims learn about the Quran through a combination of traditional and modern methods. The goal is to achieve a profound understanding of the divine message, enabling them to incorporate its teachings into their daily lives and deepen their spiritual connection with Allah.

# Chapter 4

# The Five Pillars of Islam

The five pillars of Islam uphold the spiritual life of Muslims around the world, providing guidance, structure, and a profound sense of purpose. With unwavering dedication and sincere commitment, adherents of Islam embrace these five timeless principles.

Rooted in the teachings of the Prophet Muhammad, these pillars serve as the framework for faith, worship, and righteous conduct, directing the lives of believers towards harmony with the divine and compassion for fellow human beings. Each pillar, distinctive in its nature, is like a separate thread intricately woven into the fabric of Islamic practice, creating a tapestry of devotion and righteousness.

Through the observance of these pillars, believers construct a pathway of devotion, selflessness, and unwavering faith, fulfilling the ultimate goal of submitting to the will of Allah and nurturing a righteous, fulfilled existence.

The five pillars are:

- Shahada (faith)
- Salah (prayer)
- Zakat (almsgiving)
- Sawm (fasting)
- Hajj (pilgrimage)

## Shahada

Shahada, the declaration of faith, stands as one of the five pillars of Islam, serving as a cornerstone upon which the entire structure of the religion is built. Rooted in the Arabic word "shahid," which means "to witness," Shahada bears profound significance to millions of Muslims worldwide, providing a clear and unifying statement of belief, devotion, and commitment.

At its essence, Shahada is a simple but powerful declaration that there is no deity worthy of worship except Allah, and that Muhammad is His final messenger. It serves as a testament to the unique oneness of Allah and affirming the role of Prophet Muhammad as the divinely chosen guide for humanity. Through the act of reciting these words, Muslims openly acknowledge their complete devotion to Allah and their acceptance of Prophet Muhammad's teachings and guidance.

For Muslims, Shahada is not just an empty recitation of words; it represents a deeply personal and life-altering commitment. By reciting the Shahada, individuals officially embrace Islam and join the global community of believers. It marks the beginning of a spiritual journey that includes the pursuit of righteousness, obedience to Allah's commandments, and adherence to the teachings of the Quran and the Hadith.

Shahada serves as a constant reminder of the unity and universality of Islam. Regardless of one's race, nationality, or social status, the declaration of faith unifies Muslims in their shared belief in Allah and the prophethood of Muhammad. It transcends borders and cultures, creating a vibrant and inclusive global community of believers who strive to obey Allah and seek His pleasure above all else.

Moreover, Shahada carries immense weight in the lives of Muslims. It serves as a guiding principle, encouraging believers to adhere to a moral and ethical code. By affirming their faith, Muslims commit to living a life of righteousness, integrity, and compassion. The Shahada inspires believers to uphold justice, promote peace, and offer kindness to others, embodying the values that Prophet Muhammad exemplified throughout his life.

Shahada also has a transformative effect on an individual's relationship with Allah. By continuously reaffirming their belief in His oneness and the status of Prophet Muhammad, Muslims strengthen their spiritual connection with their Creator. It serves as a daily reminder that Allah is always watching and that one's actions should always be in line with His teachings. This proclamation of faith becomes an intimate conversation between the individual and Allah, reinforcing the sense of accountability and the pursuit of spiritual growth.

Furthermore, Shahada often plays a pivotal role in important milestones throughout a Muslim's life. From birth to death and every moment in between, the declaration of faith remains a constant companion. It is recited at the beginning of the Adhan (call to prayer) and enters the ears of newborns to initiate them into the Muslim community. It is whispered as a final testament during the last moments of life, providing solace and a sense of peace.

## Salah

Salah, or prayer, is one of the five pillars of Islam. Derived from the Arabic word "صلاة" (salāh), which means to connect, Salah serves as a form of communication between the individual and the divine.

Prayer is a manifestation of a Muslim's faith and devotion to Allah. It is a means of seeking guidance, solace, and spiritual growth. Muslims believe that Salah was ordained upon them by Allah Himself through the Prophet Muhammad, making it a direct, personal connection to the divine. The regular performance of Salah allows Muslims to affirm their allegiance to Allah and remain steadfast in their commitment to Him.

The practice of Salah is not limited to a mere recitation of prescribed verses or a series of physical movements. It encompasses the mind, body, and soul during the spiritual journey during each prayer. It serves as a moment of reflection, relinquishing worldly concerns and focusing solely on the divine presence. As Muslims stand in prayer, their hearts and minds are directed towards Allah, seeking His forgiveness, guidance, and blessings.

Salah is performed five times a day, following a set schedule that reflects the rhythm of the day and night. The first prayer, Fajr, occurs before sunrise, reminding Muslims of the light breaking through the darkness and representing the beginning of a new day. It serves as a spiritual awakening and a call to embark on a day of righteousness and devotion.

The midday prayer, Dhuhr, marks the zenith of the sun's path. It serves as a reminder for individuals to pause amidst their busy lives and reconnect with Allah.

The afternoon prayer, Asr, reminds Muslims of the transitory nature of life and the need for constant self-reflection. This prayer allows for a contemplative pause in the day, reinforcing the significance of balancing one's temporal responsibilities with spiritual devotion.

The evening prayer, Maghrib, is performed just after sunset, as darkness gradually envelops the sky. It serves as a reminder of the fleeting nature of worldly pleasures and the need to seek solace and guidance in the divine.

Lastly, the night prayer, Isha, concludes the day by focusing on self-reflection and repentance. As individuals prepare to rest and seek solace in the embrace of sleep, they supplicate to Allah for His mercy and forgiveness.

In essence, Salah stands as a conduit between the individual and the divine. Through this act of worship, Muslims demonstrate their commitment to Allah, seeking spiritual nourishment and guidance.

It provides a framework for self-discipline, mindfulness, and the cultivation of a deep and personal relationship with the Creator.

## Zakat

Zakat, which translates to "purification" or "growth," is not only an act of charity but also a means of purifying one's wealth and supporting the less fortunate in society.

Zakat is an obligation for every financially capable Muslim, designed to ensure the equitable distribution of wealth within the community. It is rooted in the belief that wealth is a blessing and a test from Allah, and those who possess it have a responsibility to share it with those less fortunate. By giving a small percentage of their surplus wealth, Muslims aim to purify and grow both their own souls and the society in which they live.

According to Islamic teachings, Zakat is levied on certain types of wealth, such as cash, gold, silver, and agricultural produce, once they reach a minimum threshold known as the nisab. This threshold is calculated annually based on the current value of these assets. Muslims who possess wealth above the nisab are obligated to give 2.5% of their annual surplus to those in need.

Zakat holds immense significance in Islam as it addresses economic inequality and fosters a sense of social responsibility. It serves as a powerful reminder for Muslims to remember the blessings bestowed upon them and to share their wealth with those who are struggling. Through Zakat, Muslims contribute to the welfare and development of their community, ensuring that no one is left behind.

The distribution of Zakat is guided by specific principles outlined in Islamic jurisprudence. It is usually given to eight categories of recipients, referred to as "asnaf," which include the poor, the destitute, those in debt, and individuals striving in the path of Allah. Additionally, Zakat can be utilized for various purposes such as healthcare, education, and supporting sustainable development initiatives. Muslim scholars and charitable organizations play a vital role in collecting and organizing Zakat funds to ensure they reach those who truly need them.

Zakat is not just a financial obligation; it is a transformative act that shapes the character of the giver. By parting with their wealth, Muslims cultivate qualities such as generosity, empathy, and gratitude. It is through acts of selflessness and kindness that individuals find fulfillment and spiritual growth. Zakat teaches the importance of detachment from material possessions, reminding Muslims that true wealth lies not in material possessions but in the richness of the heart.

Furthermore, Zakat fosters a sense of unity within the Muslim community. It brings people together, regardless of their social or economic status, reinforcing the bonds of brotherhood and sisterhood. The act of giving and receiving allows Muslims to experience firsthand the interconnectedness of humanity. Through Zakat, bridges are built between individuals of different backgrounds, fostering a collective consciousness of compassion and social justice.

In today's world, where poverty and inequality persist, Zakat remains as relevant as ever. It is a powerful tool for addressing systemic issues and empowering those who have been marginalized. By fulfilling their Zakat obligations, Muslims actively participate in building a more just and equitable society, transcending boundaries and working towards the betterment of all.

## Sawn

Sawn, or fasting, is a religious obligation that requires abstaining from food, drink, and other physical needs from dawn until sunset during the holy month of Ramadan. This act of self-discipline and devotion is believed to bring spiritual purification, increased empathy, and a deeper relationship with Allah.

The practice of Sawn is rooted in the traditions and teachings of Prophet Muhammad, who first received the revelations of the Quran during the month of Ramadan. It is a time of reflection, restraint, and self-control for Muslims, where they channel their focus towards their faith, personal growth, and connecting with their Creator.

The significance of fasting goes beyond mere abstention from food and drink. It transcends the physical and takes on a spiritual dimension. Muslims engage in Sawn as an act of worship, not just to conform to religious norms but to also attain a state of increased piety and closeness to Allah. By denying themselves physical necessities, Muslims aim to purify their hearts, control their desires, and attain a heightened sense of empathy for those less fortunate.

Fasting is not exclusive to Islam, however, as many other religious and spiritual traditions incorporate it as a means of achieving spiritual growth and self-control. In Islam, the practice of Sawn goes beyond dietary restrictions and encompasses avoiding sinful behavior, such as lying, backbiting, and engaging in arguments. Muslims are encouraged to maintain a peaceful demeanor, actively seek forgiveness, and engage in acts of charity during Ramadan.

Sawn provides an opportunity for Muslims to reflect on their lives, both on an individual and communal level. It encourages self-evaluation and self-improvement, prompting Muslims to examine their actions and intentions. By refraining from physical indulgence, Muslims are able to redirect their attention towards their internal world, seeking guidance from Allah and fostering spiritual growth. The daily breaking of the fast, known as Iftar, is a time for Muslims to gather with family and friends, sharing meals and strengthening their bonds as a community.

Beyond its spiritual significance, Sawn also holds health benefits. It allows the body to detoxify and rejuvenate, as the digestive system gets a much-needed break. Muslims are encouraged to consume nutritious meals during Suhoor, the pre-dawn meal, and Iftar to ensure they receive the necessary nutrients. Many Muslims view Ramadan as an opportunity to adopt healthier lifestyles, incorporating exercise and proper nutrition into their daily routine.

The observance of Sawn is an inclusive practice that unites Muslims of all walks of life. It transcends age, gender, nationality, or social status, as believers from diverse backgrounds gather in mosques or community centers to break their fasts together. This communal aspect of Ramadan fosters a sense of unity, empathy, and support, strengthening the bonds between individuals and leaving a lasting impact on communities.

## Hajj

Hajj is an obligatory pilgrimage that every able-bodied and financially capable Muslim must undertake at least once in their lifetime. It is a sacred journey that takes place in the month of Dhu al-Hijjah, the final month of the Islamic lunar calendar, and is an act of devotion and surrender to the will of Allah.

The significance of Hajj can be traced back to the time of the Prophet Muhammad, who performed the pilgrimage in the year 632 CE. It was during this pilgrimage that the Prophet delivered his farewell sermon, outlining the fundamental principles of Islam and emphasizing the importance of unity, equality, and justice among all Muslims.

The journey of Hajj begins with the intention and preparations of the pilgrim. It is not just a physical journey, but also a spiritual one that requires immense dedication and preparation. Pilgrims must purify their hearts and minds, seeking forgiveness for past sins, and striving to attain spiritual enlightenment.

The first of the essential rites of Hajj is the wearing of the ihram, a two-piece simple white garment that symbolizes purity and equality.

The ihram serves as a visual reminder that all pilgrims, regardless of their background or wealth, stand as equals before Allah. It is a powerful reminder of the unity and brotherhood that exists among Muslims.

Upon entering the city of Mecca, the spiritual heart of Islam, pilgrims perform the Tawaf, which involves circumambulating the Kaaba, the cubic structure believed to be the first house of worship built by Prophet Ibrahim and his son Ismail. The Tawaf represents the devotion and commitment Muslims have towards the worship of Allah and reminds them of the importance of unity in their faith.

Following the Tawaf, pilgrims embark on the Safa-Marwa journey, reenacting the actions of Hajar, the wife of Prophet Ibrahim, who ran between the hills of Safa and Marwa in search of water for her infant son, Ismail. This ritual symbolizes the steadfastness, patience, and trust in Allah that Muslims should aspire to emulate in their lives.

One of the most powerful and emotionally charged moments of Hajj occurs on the ninth day of Dhu al-Hijjah, known as the Day of Arafah. It is on this day that millions of pilgrims gather on the plains of Arafat, standing in prayer and supplication, seeking forgiveness and mercy from Allah. It is believed that on this day, Allah's mercy descends upon the pilgrims, forgiving their sins and bestowing blessings upon them.

From Arafat, the pilgrimage continues to Muzdalifah, where pilgrims spend the night, collecting pebbles for the next ritual known as the Stoning of the Devil. This ritual involves throwing seven pebbles at three stone pillars, symbolizing the rejection of evil and the refusal to be led astray by Satan's temptations.

The following days witness the sacrifice of an animal, the shaving of the head or trimming of hair, and the final Tawaf and Sa'i, which symbolize the completion of the pilgrimage and the return to a renewed spiritual state.

Hajj is not simply a ritualistic exercise; it is a transformative experience that aims to purify the soul, strengthen one's faith, and foster a sense of community among Muslims. The gathering of millions of people from diverse backgrounds and cultures showcases the universality of Islam and reinforces the principle of unity and equality of all believers.

In addition to its religious significance, Hajj also serves as a time of reflection and introspection for individuals. It is an opportunity to detach oneself from the distractions of daily life and focus solely on the worship of Allah, seeking His forgiveness and guidance.

In conclusion, the five pillars of Islam stand tall as the foundation of a devout Muslim's life, guiding them on a righteous path toward spiritual fulfillment and connection with Allah. Honoring the Shahada, embracing Salah, contributing to Zakat, undertaking the fast of Ramadan, and embarking on the pilgrimage to Mecca exemplify the core principles of Islam.

These pillars not only provide a framework for worship and devotion but also emphasize the importance of faith, unity, generosity, self-control, and humility. By observing these pillars, Muslims foster a deep sense of discipline, mindfulness, and gratitude, nurturing a harmonious relationship with both their fellow human beings and the Divine.

# Chapter 5

# Beliefs in Islam

Muslims have a rich and diverse set of beliefs rooted in the teachings of the Quran, their holy book, and the Hadith, the sayings and actions of the Prophet Muhammad.

Islamic belief incorporates the concept of a divine decree, known as Qadar. Muslims believe that everything that happens in the world, both good and bad, is predestined by Allah's wisdom and sovereign will. This belief gives Muslims a sense of reassurance in times of hardship and encourages them to strive for righteousness while accepting life's challenges with gratitude and trust in Allah's plan.

Muslims also adhere to a moral and ethical code of conduct known as adab. This code emphasizes honesty, integrity, compassion, kindness, fairness, and respect for self and others. Adhering to these virtues is seen as a means to purifying the soul and attaining spiritual growth.

## Oneness of God

The belief in the oneness of God, known as Tawhid, is a fundamental principle in the Islamic faith. It serves as the cornerstone of the Muslim belief system, emphasizing the monotheistic nature of Islam. Tawhid encompasses the belief that there is only one God, Allah, who is all-powerful, all-knowing, and the creator of the universe.

Within the Islamic tradition, the oneness of God is not simply a theoretical concept, but a deeply spiritual and practical foundation that shapes the lives of Muslims. It is a belief that unites Muslims and forms the basis for their worship, devotion, and ethical conduct.

Muslims firmly believe that there is no deity worthy of worship except Allah. They reject any form of polytheism or the attribution of any partners or associates with Allah. This understanding is beautifully captured in the declaration of faith, known as the Shahada, which Muslims recite daily: "There is no deity except Allah, and Muhammad is the Messenger of Allah."

This belief in the oneness of God brings immense comfort to Muslims, providing them with the assurance that Allah is the ultimate source of guidance, mercy, and sustenance. Muslims recognize that Allah is the sole creator and controller of the universe, and that no one has any authority or power independent of Him. This understanding instills a sense of humility and reliance upon Allah in all aspects of life.

Moreover, the belief in the oneness of God serves as a guide in the moral and ethical conduct of Muslims. Since Allah is the only ultimate judge, Muslims understand that they are accountable to Him alone. This belief fosters a strong sense of responsibility and encourages Muslims to uphold justice, kindness, and compassion in their interactions with others.

Tawhid also emphasizes the unity and equality of all humanity. Muslims believe that all people are created by Allah, regardless of their nationality, race, or social status. This understanding promotes a strong sense of brotherhood and encourages Muslims to treat others with dignity, respect, and fairness.

In practical terms, the belief in the oneness of God is manifested in various aspects of Muslim life. Muslims engage in five daily prayers, or Salah, to establish a direct connection with Allah. They also engage in fasting during the holy month of Ramadan, as an act of worship and self-discipline.

Muslims are encouraged to study the Quran, which serves as a guide for moral conduct and spiritual growth. The Quran repeatedly emphasizes the oneness of God, reminding Muslims to recognize and worship Allah alone.

## Prophethood

Prophethood holds a significant place among the core beliefs of Islam, serving as a cornerstone of faith for Muslims around the world. The concept of prophethood derives from the belief that Allah, the one true God, appointed chosen individuals to guide and convey His divine message to humanity. These individuals, known as prophets, were bestowed with exceptional qualities, wisdom, and communication skills to fulfill their sacred mission.

In Islam, there are several prominent prophets mentioned in the Quran and Hadiths. Some of the well-known prophets include:

- Adam (Adam)
- Noah (Nuh)
- Abraham (Ibrahim)
- Moses (Musa)
- Jesus (Isa)
- Muhammad, considered the final prophet

In addition to these major prophets, there are also many other prophets mentioned in Islamic literature, such as Hud, Saleh, Ishmael, Isaac, Jacob, Joseph, David, Solomon, and many more. There are 25 prophets mentioned in the Quran, although the total is believed to be around 124,000. Each prophet was sent by Allah to guide humanity and convey His message.

The prophets are revered and respected for their unwavering devotion to God and their tireless efforts in guiding their people towards the path of righteousness.

As we know, the most prominent prophet in Islam is the Prophet Muhammad. Muslims greatly revere and love him as the final messenger of Allah.

The prophets are believed to possess extraordinary qualities that set them apart from ordinary individuals. They were divinely chosen, free from major sins, and bestowed with an extraordinary level of wisdom and insight. Their purity of heart and character enabled them to be a channel for divine revelation, receiving guidance directly from God. They had the ability to perform miracles as a sign of their authenticity and to provide spiritual guidance to their people.

The prophets not only conveyed the message of monotheism but also guided their people in matters of ethics, morality, and social justice. They encouraged the pursuit of knowledge and urged their followers to be compassionate, just, and honest in their dealings with others. The prophets' teachings were comprehensive and encompassed various aspects of life, such as personal conduct, worship, family relations, economics, and governance. Their wisdom and guidance laid the foundations for Islamic principles, fostering a harmonious society based on justice and respect for all.

Each prophet had a unique mission and was sent to a specific community or nation, depending on the prevailing circumstances and needs of that era. Their role was to guide their people back to the path of righteousness, warn them of the consequences of straying from God's commandments, and provide hope and encouragement during times of hardship.

Muslims hold a deep reverence for the prophets and consider it an essential part of their faith to believe in all the prophets and their teachings. They are seen as the embodiment of righteousness and the epitome of moral values. Muslims strive to emulate the prophets' qualities and teachings in their everyday lives, seeking to deepen their connection with God and contribute positively to society.

## Sacred Texts

The Quran stands as the primary and most revered source of Islamic teachings. As such, this remarkable book is believed to possess divine authority and infallibility, and is esteemed as a timeless message from the Creator Himself.

Muslims hold the utmost respect for the Quran, treating it with reverence and handling it with clean hands. Its verses are often recited melodiously during prayer, and in many Muslim households, copies of the Quran are placed in prominent locations as a symbol of devotion and blessing. The deep spiritual connection believers forge with this sacred text fosters a profound sense of unity within the global Muslim community.

While the Quran holds a unique position of authority, it is not the sole sacred text in Islam. Islamic tradition recognizes several other revered writings that contribute to understanding the faith. The Hadith, for example, comprises the sayings, actions, and approvals of the Prophet Muhammad. Collected and compiled meticulously by scholars, the Hadith offers practical and contextual guidance beyond the Quran, shedding light on the Prophet's exemplary behavior and teachings.

Another notable text is the Sunnah, which encompasses the actions and teachings of the Prophet Muhammad as observed and reported by his companions. It serves as a valuable source for understanding the application of Islamic principles in various domains of life, including worship, family, commerce, and governance.

Furthermore, Islamic literature boasts a rich collection of philosophical, jurisprudential, and mystical texts that have shaped the intellectual discourse within the faith. From the works of influential scholars like Al-Farabi, Ibn Rushd, and Al-Ghazali, to the mystical poetry of Rumi, Islamic literature encompasses a vast array of wisdom, offering diverse perspectives and insights to the faithful.

The centrality of sacred texts in Islam reflects the profound importance placed on knowledge, education, and spiritual growth. By adhering to the teachings contained within these writings, Muslims strive to cultivate a deep and intimate relationship with Allah, purify their hearts, refine their character, and positively impact the world around them.

## Angels

In Islamic theology, angels hold a significant place as celestial beings created by Allah. They are unique entities, created with sublime purity and perfect obedience to carry out the divine commands from their creator. Islam teaches that angels are part of the unseen world, beyond the realm of human senses, and play a vital role in the cosmic order and the affairs of the universe.

Muslims believe that Allah created angels from pure light or spiritual essence, free from any humanly limitations or desires. These celestial beings possess no physical form, yet their existence is profound and powerful. They serve in various roles assigned by Allah, functioning as messengers, protectors, recorders, and observers of human beings and their actions.

The most significant angel in Islam is Jibril (Gabriel), known as the "trusted spirit" who brings revelations to the Prophets. He is the angel who conveyed the Quran to the last and final Prophet, Muhammad. Jibril plays a pivotal role as the intermediary between Allah and humankind, delivering divine guidance and knowledge throughout the ages.

Another prominent angel in Islamic belief is Mika'il (Michael), assigned as the guardian of natural phenomena such as rain, harvests, and sustenance. He is responsible for the distribution of blessings and provisions to all creatures on earth. Mika'il epitomizes Allah's mercy and benevolence, ensuring that the cycles of creation continue to function harmoniously.

Muslims also believe in Israfil, the angel entrusted with the task of sounding the trumpet on the Day of Judgment, signaling the end of the world and the resurrection of all souls. Israfil's role in the eschatological events signifies the continuity and inevitability of cosmic justice and divine decrees.

Additionally, angels serve as the bearers of Allah's commandments and act as scribes, recording the deeds of individuals in a book called "The Book of Deeds." They meticulously record every action, word, and intention in an individual's life, forming an unalterable record that will be presented on the Day of Judgment. This belief in angelic recorders emphasizes the importance of ethical conduct and accountability in Muslim life.

Islam teaches that every individual is assigned two angels known as Kiraman Katibin. These angels accompany humans throughout their lives, recording their good and bad deeds in the Book of Deeds. These angelic scribes provide constant companionship, offering support and protection, and praying for the prosperity and guidance of those they are assigned with.

Muslims believe that angels also carry out specific duties in the realm of the unseen. They guard and protect humans, preventing unseen harm from reaching them. Every believer has a guardian angel who keeps watch, guiding and protecting them from evil influences. Additionally, angels are present during congregational prayers, surrounding the worshipers and seeking forgiveness for them from Allah.

In Islam, the belief in angels provides an appreciation for the divine workings in the world. It instills a sense of wonder and humility, reminding Muslims that they are part of a grand cosmic order overseen by Allah and His celestial messengers. This belief encourages devout Muslims to adopt virtuous and righteous behavior, always conscious of the divine presence and the accountability of their actions.

## Day of Judgment

The Day of Judgment, also known as the Last Day, is a significant event in the Islamic faith. Muslims believe it is a day when all humankind will stand before Allah, the Almighty, to be held accountable for their actions and to receive their final judgment.

According to Islamic teachings, the signs of the Day of Judgment are numerous and have been described in great detail in religious texts. These signs include both minor signs that have occurred throughout history and major signs that will take place closer to the end of time. Examples of minor signs include the spread of injustice, the neglect of prayers, and the increase in arguing and disputes. Major signs, on the other hand, involve the appearance of the Dajjal (Antichrist), the return of Jesus, and the emergence of Yajuj and Majuj (Gog and Magog).

On the Day of Judgment, Muslims believe that individuals will be resurrected, their bodies reassembled, and their souls reconnected, to face their ultimate fate. It is important to note that Islam emphasizes the belief in bodily resurrection as a fundamental aspect of the faith. Every person will be held accountable for their deeds, both big and small, as Allah's ultimate justice will prevail.

The judgment of each individual will be based on their actions and the intentions behind them. Muslims believe that Allah is the All-Knowing and will judge each individual fairly, taking into account their circumstances and intentions. It is believed that even the smallest of actions, words, and thoughts will be evaluated and weighed. The concept of mercy is also a vital aspect of Islamic belief, and it is believed that Allah's mercy will ultimately determine the fate of individuals.

Muslims believe that there are two possible outcomes on the Day of Judgment: paradise or hellfire. Paradise, or Jannah, is described as a place of eternal bliss, where the righteous will be rewarded for their faith and good deeds. It is a place of unimaginable beauty, with rivers of milk, honey, and wine flowing, and where every desire is fulfilled. Conversely, hellfire, or Jahannam, is described as a place of intense punishment for those who chose to disbelieve or commit evil acts. It is a place of indescribable torment and suffering, where the disobedient will be confined.

The Day of Judgment holds great significance for Muslims, serving as a reminder of the consequences of their actions in this world. It encourages believers to live a righteous life, following the guidance provided by the Quran and the teachings of the Prophet Muhammad. Muslims believe that the Day of Judgment should inspire them to constantly strive for good deeds, seek forgiveness for their shortcomings, and treat others with kindness and compassion.

While the concept of the Day of Judgment may appear daunting, it is ultimately a reminder of Allah's justice, mercy, and wisdom. It serves as a testament to the belief that our actions in this world have consequences, both in this life and the hereafter. Muslims view the Day of Judgment as a source of hope, as they have faith in Allah's infinite mercy and seek His forgiveness and guidance throughout their lives.

In conclusion, exploring the main beliefs of Islam provides a profound understanding of this ancient and rich faith. The layered teachings that form the foundation of Islam are rooted in monotheism, divine mercy, and the pursuit of righteousness.

## CHAPTER 6

# Worship and Rituals in Islam

Rituals play a fundamental role in the lives of Muslims, serving as a tangible manifestation of their religious devotion and commitment. These rituals are deeply ingrained in their daily routines, connecting them to their faith, community, and the divine.

In this section, we will explore the importance of rituals in Muslim life, shedding light on their spiritual, social, and psychological significance.

Strengthening the Spiritual Connection

Rituals form a powerful means for Muslims to deepen their spiritual connection with Allah (God) and strengthen their faith. The daily five prayers, known as Salah, serve as a constant reminder of their commitment to worship and submission to God. These ritual prayers involve physical movements accompanied by recitation of verses from the Quran, such as bowing, prostrating, and standing in unity with the Muslim community. This rhythmic engagement fosters a sense of tranquility, humility, and spiritual elevation, enabling Muslims to seek solace in their relationship with Allah.

**Establishing Discipline and Self-control**

Muslim rituals, particularly fasting during the holy month of Ramadan, instill discipline and self-control among individuals. Through abstaining from food, water, and other physical needs from sunrise to sunset, Muslims learn to conquer their desires and develop self-restraint. This practice extends beyond the month of

Ramadan, impacting their daily lives, ensuring they are mindful of their actions and strive to avoid indulgence in sinful behavior. Such discipline empowers Muslims to lead a balanced and morally upright life.

**Unity and Social Cohesion**

Rituals in Islam often involve congregational worship, fostering a strong sense of unity and social bonding among adherents. The weekly Friday prayer at the mosque, known as Jummah, serves as a gathering point for Muslims to come together, perform the congregational prayer, listen to the sermon, and engage in community affairs. This regular interaction fosters connections, friendship, and collective responsibility, thus reinforcing social cohesion within the Muslim community. Rituals also provide a platform for Muslims to celebrate diverse occasions, such as Eid al-Fitr and Eid al-Adha, encouraging communal festivities and reinforcing a sense of belonging.

**Emotional Well-being and Psychological Growth**

Rituals in Muslim life contribute significantly to emotional well-being and psychological growth. Engaging in acts like reciting the Quran, supplicating to Allah, and performing pilgrimage to Mecca (Hajj), instills a sense of peace, serenity, and spiritual fulfillment. These practices provide solace during times of distress, anxiety, or grief, as Muslims find comfort in seeking solace from their Creator. Moreover, rituals promote mindfulness, self-reflection, and introspection, allowing individuals to gain a deeper understanding of themselves and their purpose in life.

The importance of rituals in Muslim life cannot be overstated. These practices serve as a visible expression of devotion, offering Muslims spirituality, discipline, unity, and emotional well-being. Rituals form the building blocks of Islam, fostering a sense of connectedness with Allah and strengthening the bonds within the Muslim community.

## Adhan – Call to Prayer

Adhan, also known as the Islamic call to prayer, holds immense significance in the lives of Muslims around the world. This ritual, performed five times a day, serves as a gentle reminder for believers to pause their worldly affairs and turn their attention towards the worship of Allah, the Almighty.

The adhan serves as a unifying force for the Muslim community, eliminating the barriers of language, nationality, and ethnicity. Regardless of where one may be in the world, upon hearing the adhan, Muslims are reminded that they are part of something larger than themselves—a global ummah, or community, of believers. This sense of unity and belonging strengthens the bonds among Muslims and helps foster a collective identity that transcends individual differences.

Beyond its unifying nature, the adhan serves as a spiritual wakeup call, urging Muslims to reorient their priorities towards their relationship with Allah. In the hustle and bustle of everyday life, it is easy to get caught up in the material world and lose sight of the ultimate purpose of our existence—to worship and serve our Creator. The adhan acts as a gentle reminder to pause, reflect, and reconnect with the Divine.

The melodious recitation of the adhan and its rhythmic flow have a calming effect on the hearts and minds of believers. The beautiful words and phrases of the adhan, recited by a talented muezzin, create an atmosphere of peace, tranquility, and spiritual serenity. It is no wonder that even non-Muslims can appreciate the soothing sound of the adhan echoing through the air, resonating with a sense of divine presence.

Moreover, the adhan acts as a beacon of hope and a call for justice. It reminds Muslims of their duty to stand against oppression and injustice, as it proclaims "Allahu Akbar" (Allah is the greatest), reaffirming the belief that no power or authority can surpass that of the Almighty. It is a reminder for believers to strive for justice and righteousness both individually and collectively, as they are accountable to Allah for their actions.

The adhan also serves as a timekeeping mechanism, ensuring that Muslims remain mindful of their daily obligations within the Islamic faith. By calling the adhan at specific intervals throughout the day, it prompts Muslims to pause their activities and engage in prayer, allowing for a spiritual recharge amidst the busyness of life. This regularity in performing the adhan helps maintain a structured daily routine, reinforcing the importance of maintaining a balanced life between worldly affairs and spiritual obligations.

## Wudu

Wudu, also known as ablution, serves as a fundamental ritual in Islam. It is a purification process that Muslims undertake before performing their prayers or engaging in acts of worship.

The act of Wudu involves the washing of specific body parts in a particular order, beginning with the hands. As water cascades over the fingertips, palms, and wrists, it symbolizes a physical and spiritual cleansing, a renewal of one's inner self. With each splash of water, Muslims strive to purify themselves not just externally, but internally as well, preparing their hearts and minds to connect with the divine.

From the hands, the flow of water makes its way to the mouth and nose. Here, Muslims gently rinse their mouths and inhale water into their nostrils, carefully expelling it. This action signifies the elimination of impurities, both physical and verbal, ensuring one's words and breath remain pure. As the water clears the sinus cavities, it brings a sense of clarity and focus to one's prayerful intentions.

Next, the face, the window to the soul, is gently washed, ensuring that every corner is touched by the cool stream of water. With this simple act, Muslims strive not only to purify the physical exterior but also to cleanse the deeper emotions and stresses that may cloud their hearts. The sensation of water trickling down the face becomes a symbol of tranquility, allowing believers to approach their prayers with a calm and serene countenance.

Moving on, attention shifts to the arms, where water flows from the fingertips up to the elbows, sweeping away the weariness and burdens of worldly pursuits. With each stroke of water, Muslims seek to renew their commitment to righteous actions, striving to extend their hands in acts of kindness and compassion towards all of humanity.

The act of wiping one's head with wet hands follows, symbolizing humility and submission to the will of Allah. As the fingers glide gently across the scalp, Muslims empty their minds of worldly distractions, inviting a state of reflection and spiritual clarity. This mindful act helps believers to redirect their focus towards the Divine, preparing for a deeply meaningful connection in prayer.

Lastly, Wudu concludes with the washing of the feet, making its way from the toes to the ankles. By cleansing the feet, Muslims honor the connection between all of creation, taking steps on the path of righteousness with a renewed sense of purpose. The cool water massaging the tired soles becomes a reminder to tread lightly on this earth, treating every step as an opportunity to spread peace and love.

Wudu is not merely a religious obligation, but a deep-rooted spiritual practice that holds the power to transform hearts and minds. It acts as a reminder to Muslims that every aspect of their being must be elevated and purified in preparation for communion with their Creator.

## Daily Prayer

At dawn, the first of the five daily prayers, Fajr, is performed. Facing the direction of the Kaaba in Makkah, the holiest site in Islam, Muslims bow down in unity, setting aside the preoccupations of the world and turning their attention toward God. This ritual prayer encourages mindfulness and a sense of humility, reminding believers of their transient nature and the eternal presence of the divine.

Throughout the day, Muslims remain conscious of their spiritual connection and engage in Dhikr, the practice of reciting the praises of Allah. Whether through prayer beads, silent repetition, or simply uttering phrases like "SubhanAllah" (glory be to God) or "Alhamdulillah" (praise be to God), these moments of remembrance help maintain a constant connection to the divine.

As the sun reaches its peak, the midday prayer, known as Dhuhr, calls the believers back to their places of worship. This prayer serves as a reminder to break away from worldly distractions and seek solace in communing with the Creator. It not only reinforces the spiritual bond but also provides an opportunity for introspection and reorientation towards sacred values.

The afternoon prayer, Asr, follows Dhuhr and serves as a way to interrupt the bustling rhythm of daily life. As Muslims pause once again, they find tranquility in submission to God's will. This ritual, like the others, helps to keep believers steadfast, reminding them that despite the transient nature of worldly matters, the relationship with the divine remains constant.

As the day turns to dusk, the Maghrib prayer beckons. By this time, the sun has set, casting its warm glow on the horizon, and Muslims gather to seek divine blessings in their evening worship. This prayer represents gratitude for the day's blessings and serves as a moment to reflect on one's deeds and seek forgiveness for any missteps.

Finally, the day ends with the Isha prayer. As darkness envelopes the world, the believers come together as a community to offer their final act of devotion before retiring to their homes. This prayer symbolizes surrender to the night, embracing the serenity and peace that accompany sleep, with the hope of awakening refreshed and renewed the next day.

## Jumu'ah (Friday)

Friday, known as Jumu'ah in Islam, holds immense significance in the lives of Muslims worldwide. Considered as the holiest day of the week, it serves as a time for spiritual rejuvenation, communal worship, and reflection on the teachings of Islam. Its importance stems from both religious and historical factors, making it a day of deep reverence and devotion for Muslims.

From a religious perspective, Friday holds a special place due to its mention in the Quran. In Surah Al-Jumu'ah, Allah states, "O you who have believed, when [the adhan] is called for the prayer on the day of Jumu'ah [Friday], then proceed to the remembrance of Allah and leave trade. That is better for you, if you only knew" (62:9). This verse emphasizes the obligation of Muslims to attend the Friday congregational prayer and engage in the remembrance of Allah.

The Friday congregational prayer, also known as Salat al-Jumu'ah, is a significant aspect of Islam. It is obligatory for Muslim men to attend this prayer if they are physically able. This prayer holds communal value, bringing together Muslims from diverse backgrounds to worship and learn together. It fosters a sense of unity, brotherhood, and sisterhood, strengthening the bonds of the Muslim community.

During the Friday sermon, known as Khutbah, the imam addresses the congregation, delivering a sermon that is both educational and motivational. This sermon serves as a means of imparting Islamic knowledge, guidance, and reminders to the worshippers. It provides an opportunity for individuals to reflect on their faith and seek spiritual growth, enhancing their understanding of Islamic principles and teachings.

Besides the religious aspects, the historical significance of Friday can also be traced back to the time of the Prophet Muhammad. The Prophet used to lay great emphasis on Friday, highlighting its importance as a day of worship and gathering. He would give sermons and offer prayers on this day, setting an example for his followers to follow.

Furthermore, Friday offers Muslims a chance to seek forgiveness and repentance. It is believed that during this day, one's prayers for forgiveness are more likely to be answered by Allah. It serves as a reminder of the continuous need for self-reflection and improvement. Muslims are encouraged to spend time in reciting the Quran, engaging in charitable acts, and seeking forgiveness for their sins.

Beyond its religious and historical significance, Friday also provides Muslims with a much-needed break from the demands of everyday life. It serves as a day to detach from worldly concerns, focus on their faith, and recharge spiritually. This break allows Muslims to rejuvenate their minds, bodies, and souls, enabling them to enter the following week with renewed energy and purpose.

## Islamic Funerals

Islamic funerals are a solemn and significant aspect of Muslim culture and tradition. They are a time for family, friends, and community members to come together to mourn, pay respects, and honor the deceased.

In Islamic tradition, it is preferred to bury the deceased as soon as possible after death. The Islamic concept of death views it as a transition from one life to the next, and the deceased are believed to be in a state of waiting until they are laid to rest. It is therefore considered a matter of urgency to complete the burial process promptly.

According to Islamic teachings, the ideal time for burial is within 24 hours after death. This practice is derived from the practice of the Prophet Muhammad and his companions, who buried their deceased loved ones at the earliest convenience. This swift burial is intended to honor the deceased and minimize any unnecessary delay or suffering they may endure on their journey to the afterlife.

However, there are certain circumstances where the immediate burial is not possible. These may include legal requirements, such as the need for autopsies or investigations, or logistical challenges, such as obtaining permits for burial or transportation. In such cases, the burial should take place as soon as these obstacles are overcome.

It is worth noting that Islamic funerals follow specific rituals and customs. The deceased is typically washed and wrapped in a simple white shroud called a kafan. This is done by family members or the local mosque community, taking care to respect the deceased's modesty and dignity. Prayers for the deceased, known as Janazah prayers, are offered collectively by the community before proceeding to the burial site.

The timing of Islamic funerals also takes into account the practical considerations of the deceased's loved ones. It is understandable that grieving family members and friends may need time to travel or make necessary arrangements to attend the funeral. Islamic teachings emphasize the importance of support and solidarity for the grieving, thus granting some flexibility in the timing of the funeral to accommodate these factors.

Ultimately, the timing of Islamic funerals reflects the deep reverence and regard Muslim communities have for the deceased and the importance of honoring their memory. They serve as a poignant reminder of the impermanence of life and the need to prepare for the eternal journey that lies ahead.

# CHAPTER 7

# Islamic Law: Shariah

Shariah, also known as Islamic law, is a system of rules and principles derived from the teachings of the Quran and the Hadith, which are the sayings and actions of the Prophet Muhammad. Guiding the personal and public lives of Muslims, Shariah is a comprehensive framework encompassing moral, social, and legal aspects. It provides guidance on matters such as family law, criminal justice, business transactions, and even personal conduct.

**Divine Authority:**

- Shariah law is believed to originate from the divine revelation of the Quran, which Muslims consider the word of God.

- It is influenced by the Hadiths, which provide insight into the Prophet Muhammad's actions, words, and approvals.

- Muslims view Shariah law as timeless and immutable, serving as a moral compass for adherents.

**Personal Conduct:**

- Shariah law promotes personal piety and self-discipline.

- It encompasses moral values and ethical guidelines for individuals' behavior, emphasizing honesty, integrity, and humility.

- Encourages acts of kindness, respect for others, and maintaining harmonious relationships within society.

**Five Pillars of Islam:**

- Shariah law incorporates the Five Pillars of Islam: Shahada (faith), Salah (prayer), Zakat (charitable giving), Sawm (fasting), and Hajj (pilgrimage).

- These religious obligations dictate the belief, worship, and social responsibilities of Muslims, fostering spiritual growth and communal connection.

**Family Law:**

- Shariah law outlines principles for marriage and divorce, inheritance, and child custody.

- Emphasizes mutual respect and responsibilities between spouses, promoting harmony in family life.

- Provides guidelines for the equitable distribution of assets upon death, ensuring fairness among family members.

**Criminal Justice:**

- Shariah law encompasses criminal justice, aiming to deter crimes and maintain social order.

- Promotes forgiveness, rehabilitation, and restoration of rights for offenders, complemented by appropriate punishments.

- Requires the provision of evidence beyond a reasonable doubt, ensuring fair trials and protecting individuals' rights.

**Economic Principles:**

- Shariah law promotes ethical financial dealings, emphasizing fairness and discouraging exploitation.

- Prohibits the charging of interest (usury) and supports profit-sharing arrangements.

- Encourages charitable giving and the redistribution of wealth through Zakat, ensuring the welfare of the less fortunate.

**Social Welfare:**

- Shariah law encourages caring for the vulnerable members of society, including orphans, the poor, and the elderly.

- Places an obligation on Muslims to provide charitable support and engage in acts of social welfare.

- Promotes collective responsibility in addressing societal issues, fostering solidarity and compassion.

**Governance and Politics:**

- Shariah law provides principles for governance, advocating for justice, consultation, and the welfare of citizens.

- Emphasizes accountability and the rule of law, aiming to prevent corruption and ensure compliance with Islamic values.

- Recognizes the authority of Islamic scholars in interpreting and implementing Shariah principles in a contemporary context.

While Shariah provides guidelines for Muslims to lead their personal lives, it is important to note that Shariah is not a monolithic system. It allows for differences in interpretation and application, resulting in a diversity of legal practices across different Muslim-majority countries. Moreover, Shariah is not intended to be imposed on non-Muslims, as it is primarily meant for the Muslim community. Non-Muslims living within Muslim-majority countries are usually subject to their own respective personal status laws.

In recent times, certain aspects of Shariah have been subject to intense debate and scrutiny, often leading to misconceptions and stereotypes. It is crucial to approach these discussions with an open mind and a willingness to engage in dialogue. A respectful understanding of Shariah allows for a more nuanced understanding of Islam and its multifaceted legal traditions.

It is important to recognize that Shariah, like any legal system, is a human interpretation of divine guidance. It is subject to human fallibility and evolving societal contexts. As with any legal system, it is essential to ensure that the principles of justice, fairness, and respect for human rights are upheld in its application.

## Sources of Islamic Law

Shariah plays a crucial role in the lives of Muslims worldwide, guiding their personal conduct, social relationships, and governance. Understanding the sources of Islamic Law is integral in comprehending its development and application.

The primary sources of Islamic Law are the Quran and the Hadith. The Quran is considered the literal word of Allah, revealed to the Prophet Muhammad over a period of more than two decades. Its verses cover a myriad of topics, including moral guidance, worship, social interactions, and issues of personal and public conduct. Many legal principles in Islam are derived directly from the Quran's explicit directives, like the prohibition of theft or the requirement of performing prayer.

The Hadith, on the other hand, includes the sayings, actions, and approvals of the Prophet Muhammad. Complied by devoted scholars over several generations, the Hadith provides detailed guidance on various aspects of life, presenting a practical model for Muslims to emulate. Hadiths are categorized according to their level of authenticity, ensuring that reliable narrations are given more weight in legal matters. Scholars meticulously analyze and interpret Hadiths to extrapolate legal rulings and generate a deeper understanding of Islamic Law.

Ijtihad, which means "exertion of effort," is another crucial source of Islamic Law. It refers to the independent reasoning and interpretation exercised by qualified scholars, known as mujtahids. These scholars diligently study the Quran and the Hadith, employing their knowledge and expertise to derive legal rulings in new and complex situations that were not explicitly addressed in the primary sources. Ijtihad is a dynamic process that allows Islamic Law to adapt and remain relevant in contemporary times.

Another important source of Islamic Law is consensus, or ijma. It refers to the agreement of the Muslim scholarly community on a particular legal issue. This consensus is reached through scholarly discussions and deliberations, spanning multiple generations and diverse geographical locations. When a consensus is achieved, it carries significant weight in determining legal rulings.

An additional source of Islamic Law is analogical reasoning, known as qiyas. Qiyas involves applying existing legal rulings to new situations that have similar underlying principles or objectives. It allows scholars to address issues not directly addressed in the primary sources by drawing logical and coherent conclusions based on established legal precedents. Qiyas allows for flexibility and adaptability in Islamic Law, enabling it to deal with contemporary challenges.

In recent times, judicial precedents, rulings, and customary practices have also been considered as supplementary sources of Islamic Law. These sources are derived from the application of Islamic Law by courts and legal authorities across different regions and historical periods. However, their status is subject to scrutiny and verification by qualified scholars to ensure their compatibility with the primary sources.

Overall, the sources of Islamic Law provide a rich and comprehensive framework for Muslims to navigate their lives in accordance with their faith. Understanding these sources is paramount in comprehending the development and application of Islamic Law.

## Application of Shariah in Everyday Life

Shariah plays a significant role in guiding the conduct and behavior of Muslims in their everyday lives. In matters of personal conduct, Shariah outlines a set of guidelines that encompass one's relationship with oneself, family, community, and society as a whole. It encourages Muslims to lead a disciplined and virtuous life, focusing on self-reflection, self-improvement, and adhering to moral values.

For instance, in the realm of personal hygiene, the Shariah emphasizes cleanliness and purity, with rituals such as ablution (wudu) before prayer and the observance of cleanliness in daily activities. This not only promotes physical wellbeing but also serves as a reminder of the importance of maintaining a pure and focused state of mind.

Shariah also plays a vital role in family matters, guiding Muslims on various aspects of marriage, divorce, and inheritance. It promotes the institution of marriage as a bond based on mutual love, respect, and support, emphasizing the importance of maintaining harmony within the family unit. Furthermore, Shariah provides guidelines for the fair distribution of wealth and assets, ensuring that individuals are treated justly and equitably in matters of inheritance.

Beyond personal and family matters, Shariah extends its principles to issues of social justice and economic ethics. It encourages Muslims to be mindful of their interactions with others, promoting fairness, honesty, and compassion in all financial transactions. Shariah prohibits usury (Riba) and exploitative practices, encouraging ethical business dealings and responsible financial behaviors, ultimately aiming to create a more just and equitable society.

Moreover, Shariah also addresses criminal and penal matters, aiming to maintain social order and protect the well-being of individuals and communities. Its principles of justice and fairness underline the significance of due process, ensuring that individuals are treated fairly, regardless of their social standing. The goal is to deter crime, rehabilitate offenders, and foster a sense of accountability and responsibility within society.

Ultimately, the application of Shariah in everyday life varies depending on cultural, geographical, and personal circumstances. It provides Muslims with a moral compass, guiding them in making choices that align with the principles of justice, compassion, and goodness. In this way, Shariah serves not only as a legal system but also as a comprehensive framework for leading a meaningful, ethical, and fulfilling life.

CHAPTER 8

# Islamic Ethics and Morality

Ethics in Islam play a fundamental role in guiding the behavior and actions of Muslims. Rooted in the teachings of the Quran, the Hadith, and Islamic jurisprudence, Islamic ethics encompass a comprehensive moral framework that shapes the way Muslims approach various aspects of life. Let's explore the key principles and values that underpin ethical conduct in Islam, emphasizing the importance of moral responsibility and accountability.

## Foundations of Islamic Ethics

At the core of Islamic ethics lies the concept of Tawhid, the belief in the oneness of Allah (God). This belief forms the basis for the moral framework in Islam, as Muslims recognize that their actions should be guided by their devotion to God and adherence to His commands. Muslims are called upon to lead a life of righteousness and morality, as the Quran teaches that they are accountable for their deeds in this life and in the hereafter.

The Quran serves as the ultimate guidebook for Muslim ethics, providing clear guidelines on how to live a virtuous and just life. It emphasizes the importance of justice, compassion, honesty, humility, and upholding the rights and dignity of others. Muslims are encouraged to be of service to humanity, to practice self-restraint and self-discipline, and to strive for excellence in all aspects of life.

The Sunnah, which encompasses the Prophet Muhammad's teachings and actions, complements and further elucidates the ethical teachings found in the Quran. Muslims view the Prophet Muhammad as the exemplary model of ethical behavior, and his sayings and actions are considered sources of guidance for Muslims in navigating the complexities of life. The Prophet emphasized the importance of good character, kindness, fairness, and integrity, and his life serves as a practical example for Muslims to follow.

Moreover, Islamic ethics emphasizes the concept of intention or niyyah. Muslims are encouraged to perform good deeds with sincere intentions, seeking only the pleasure of Allah and not seeking recognition or praise from others. It is believed that the intention behind an action holds great significance in determining its moral value.

Islamic ethics also extends to areas such as social justice, economic ethics, environmental ethics, and ethical treatment of animals. Upholding social justice and standing up for the rights of the oppressed is considered a responsibility for Muslims, as the Quran stresses the importance of fighting injustice and striving for a society that is fair and equitable for all.

## The Pursuit of Moral Excellence

In Islam, the concept of ihsan holds tremendous significance as it encompasses the pursuit of moral excellence and inner spiritual refinement. Rooted in the teachings of the Prophet Muhammad, ihsan calls upon believers to strive for excellence in their relationship with Allah, themselves, and others.

At its core, ihsan encourages individuals to go beyond mere adherence to religious obligations and rituals. It beckons them to not only perform acts of worship, but to also do so with sincerity, excellence, and mindfulness. It encompasses the cultivation of noble traits, such as compassion, patience, humility, gratitude, and kindness—virtues that shape one's character and interactions with the world around them.

The pursuit of ihsan involves a sense of self-awareness and introspection, as individuals strive to purify their hearts and align their intentions with the pleasure of Allah. It places emphasis on acts of worship becoming a means of attaining closeness to the Divine, rather than becoming mechanical or detached rituals.

By embodying ihsan, Muslims are encouraged to extend their ethical conduct to all aspects of life. It applies to their relationships with family members, friends, colleagues, and even strangers. The recognition of the intrinsic worth of every individual, regardless of their background or beliefs, is a fundamental aspect of ihsan. This perspective fosters an environment of understanding, tolerance, and respect, thus promoting harmonious coexistence within society.

Islamic teachings remind us that ihsan is not a one-time accomplishment but a lifelong journey. It requires constant self-reflection, rectification of one's intentions, and seeking forgiveness for any shortcomings. Muslims are encouraged to strive for ihsan in all their actions, both in public and in private, realizing that they are accountable for their choices and conduct.

In the pursuit of ihsan, Islam emphasizes the importance of seeking knowledge and understanding. It encourages believers to acquire wisdom, not only through formal education but by engaging in continual learning and reflection. By doing so, individuals deepen their understanding of the principles and values that underpin moral excellence, enabling them to apply them more effectively in their daily lives.

## Justice and Fairness

In Islam, the principles of justice and fairness hold immense significance, with Adl being the Arabic term encapsulating these concepts. Adl emphasizes the need for individuals to treat others equitably, ensuring that every person is given their due rights and that no one is subjected to injustice.

At its core, Islam regards justice as not merely a social obligation but also a spiritual one, intertwining the principles of righteousness and accountability. The Quran repeatedly emphasizes the importance of justice, stating that it is a cornerstone of a righteous society. Prophet Muhammad exemplified and advocated for the highest standards of justice, treating all individuals fairly, regardless of their socio-economic status, race, or religion.

Justice in Islam extends to all spheres of life, from personal interactions to communal affairs and even within institutions of governance. Islam encourages individuals to practice justice even in the face of adversity, as the Prophet Muhammad said, "Be just, even if it is against yourselves."

Furthermore, Islam emphasizes the importance of fairness by discouraging discrimination and favoritism. Islam teaches that people should be evaluated and treated based on their actions and character, rather than their social status or any other external factors. This principle is beautifully summarized in the verse: "O you who have believed, be persistently standing firm in justice, witnesses for Allah, even if it be against yourselves or parents and relatives" (Quran, 4:135).

Islam also promotes the idea that justice should prevail in matters of law and governance. Islamic legal systems strive to uphold the principles of fairness and equity, ensuring that individuals have equal access to justice and are treated impartially. Islamic jurisprudence aims to address societal issues by taking into account the unique circumstances and context, promoting the highest standards of justice.

Adl in Islam extends beyond human interactions and encompasses the relationship between believers and their Creator. Muslims believe that Allah is the epitome of justice and that they will be held accountable for their deeds in the Hereafter. This belief serves as a moral compass, guiding individuals to consistently strive for justice and fairness in all aspects of their lives.

## Virtuous Character and Good Manners

Akhlaq, commonly referred to as good manners and virtuous character, occupies a significant place in Islam. It encompasses various aspects of behavior and conduct towards oneself, others, and the society as a whole. In Islam, cultivating a noble character and displaying good manners is not merely an encouraged practice, but rather a crucial part of a believer's journey toward attaining closeness to Allah and leading a righteous life.

One of the fundamental teachings of Islam is to embody the attributes of kindness, compassion, patience, honesty, humility, and fairness. These qualities are encouraged in every interaction, whether it be with family, friends, colleagues, or even strangers. The Prophet Muhammad himself was the epitome of virtue and set an impeccable example for his followers in terms of his manners and character.

Islam emphasizes the importance of akhlaq not only in how we treat others but also in how we conduct ourselves in private. It reminds us to be accountable for our actions and intentions, promoting integrity, sincerity, and self-discipline. Upholding virtuous character, even when no one is watching, is highly praised in Islam, as it demonstrates faithfulness and a commitment to righteousness.

Furthermore, the teachings of Islam urge believers to be kind and compassionate towards all creatures, including animals and the environment. Respecting and caring for the natural world is considered an integral part of manifesting good character. Islam promotes the idea of utilizing resources responsibly, avoiding waste, and protecting the earth for future generations.

In practicing good manners and cultivating virtuous character, Islam also emphasizes the concept of forgiveness and forbearance. Believers are encouraged to be patient when faced with challenges or adversities, to forgive others for their mistakes, and to seek reconciliation when conflicts arise. This approach fosters harmony, unity, and compassion within society, nourishing a morally conscious community.

It is important to note that akhlaq is not limited to a set of superficial actions, but rather, it stems from a genuine intent to please Allah and benefit others. Islam emphasizes the inner transformation of the heart, which then reflects in one's outward behavior. This highlights the significance of continuously striving to improve our character and to seek Allah's guidance in doing so.

## God-Consciousness and Accountability

In Islam, the concept of Taqwa plays a significant role in shaping the behavior and mindset of believers. Taqwa, often translated as God-consciousness or mindfulness, refers to cultivating a deep sense of reverence, awe, and awareness of the presence of Allah (God) in every aspect of life.

Practicing Taqwa means being mindful of one's actions, thoughts, and intentions, and aligning them with the teachings and principles of Islam. It serves as a compass that guides Muslims towards choosing righteousness and abstaining from immoral or unlawful deeds. The ultimate goal is to attain a state of purity and nearness to Allah, while constantly striving to improve one's character.

The concept of Taqwa emphasizes the accountability of individuals for their actions. Muslims believe that every deed, whether big or small, is recorded by Allah and will be accounted for in the Hereafter. This awareness fosters a sense of responsibility and encourages believers to be mindful of their behavior at all times.

Taqwa acts as a shield against heedlessness and moral decay. By cultivating this consciousness, Muslims strive to maintain integrity in their interactions with others, uphold justice, practice patience, and fulfill their obligations. It motivates believers to be honest, humble, and compassionate, not only in their worship but also in their daily dealings with fellow human beings.

Islam teaches that Taqwa is not limited to external acts of worship, but is a holistic approach encompassing inward sincerity and piety as well. It encompasses the purification of one's soul, strengthening the bond with Allah through intimate devotion, and seeking constant repentance for any wrongdoings.

Practicing Taqwa is a continuous journey that requires self-reflection, constant self-improvement, and seeking knowledge. It is an ongoing process wherein believers strive to increase their awareness, knowledge, and understanding of Allah's commandments and apply them in their lives.

## Mercy and Compassion

In Islam, the concepts of mercy and compassion hold profound significance, shaping the moral fabric of believers. As followers of the faith, adherents are encouraged to embody mercy and compassion in all aspects of their lives, towards both humans, animals, and all of Allah's creation.

Mercy, a divine attribute of Allah, is seen as a fundamental characteristic to be sought after and reflected upon by every Muslim. The Holy Quran highlights the encompassing nature of Allah's mercy, emphasizing that it extends to all beings, regardless of their beliefs or backgrounds. It is through this profound mercy that Muslims are encouraged to approach their interactions with others, manifesting forgiveness, empathy, and kindness.

Compassion, too, holds a central role in Islam's teachings. It involves not only feeling sympathy toward those who are suffering but also taking active steps to alleviate their pain and provide support. The Prophet Muhammad set an example by showing abundant compassion to all beings, irrespective of their status in society. He emphasized the importance of treating others with gentleness and consideration, promoting a culture of caring concern.

Islam teaches that acts of mercy and compassion are not limited to individuals but extend to the entire community and even the world at large. Muslims are encouraged to promote justice, alleviate poverty, and serve those in need, whether through charitable deeds or by actively striving to create a just and equitable society. By engaging in acts of mercy and compassion, believers seek to strengthen the bond between themselves, Allah, and humanity.

It is this emphasis on mercy and compassion that fosters a sense of unity and inclusivity within the Islamic faith. Muslims are reminded that every individual is deserving of mercy and compassion, regardless of their mistakes or shortcomings. Furthermore, the spirit of mercy and compassion encourages believers to engage in dialogue, seek understanding, and work towards peaceful coexistence with people of diverse backgrounds, fostering a sense of harmony and mutual respect.

## Modesty and Decency

Modesty and decency hold a significant place in the teachings of Islam, encouraging individuals to adhere to a code of conduct that reflects respect and dignity. Islam guides its followers to embrace modesty in their attitudes, appearances, and interactions, ultimately cultivating a society that values self-restraint and moral excellence.

In Islam, modesty encompasses both physical and intellectual aspects. It emphasizes the importance of modest clothing that covers the body in a manner that preserves one's modesty and guards against displaying or attracting any form of inappropriate attention. It encourages individuals to dress modestly, wearing loose-fitting and non-transparent garments that do not draw unnecessary attention to one's physical features.

Moreover, the concept of modesty extends beyond outer appearances and touches upon the way individuals speak and carry themselves. Islam encourages both men and women to display humility, speak gently, and avoid engaging in conversations that may lead to immorality or indecency. By embodying modesty in speech, Muslims strive to create an atmosphere of respect and dignity in their interactions with others.

An integral part of modesty in Islam is the establishment of strong moral values and ethical behavior. Muslims are advised to guard their thoughts and intentions, ensuring they align with righteous and virtuous principles. Islam urges individuals to uphold decency in their thoughts, deeds, and intentions, guiding them to lead a life that is pleasing to both Allah and society.

It is important to note that modesty in Islam is not exclusively imposed on women but extends to men as well. Both genders are expected to dress and conduct themselves modestly, recognizing the value of modesty in maintaining the sanctity of the individual and society as a whole. Islam promotes the idea that modesty is not a form of oppression but rather a means to attain inner peace and tranquility, fostering an environment of mutual respect and honor.

The adherence to modesty in Islam is not about stifling personal expression or suppressing one's individuality. Rather, it aims to strike a balance between personal freedoms and the responsibility to maintain a virtuous and dignified society. Islam recognizes the inherent beauty and value within each individual and encourages them to be mindful of how they present themselves to others.

By embracing the principles of modesty and decency, followers of Islam strive to create an atmosphere of purity, integrity, and compassion within their communities. It becomes a way of life that reflects the teachings of the faith, fostering a society that upholds respect, dignity, and moral excellence for all its members.

## Family Values and Relationships

Family is considered a cornerstone of society, and strong family values are highly cherished. The teachings of Islam emphasize the importance of fostering loving and nurturing relationships within the family unit. It is believed that a harmonious and united family plays a vital role in creating a healthy society.

Islam places great emphasis on the relationship between spouses. Marriage is considered a sacred bond, reflecting a partnership based on love, compassion, and mutual respect. Husbands and wives are encouraged to support and care for each other, sharing responsibilities and seeking to maintain a peaceful and loving environment within their home.

Respecting and honoring parents is highly valued in Islam. Children are taught to be obedient and show gratitude to their parents, recognizing them as their primary source of love, care, and guidance. Islam encourages maintaining close ties with extended family members as well, promoting a sense of unity and support within the larger family structure.

In Islam, forgiveness and reconciliation are also greatly emphasized. When disputes or conflicts arise within the family, Islam encourages open communication, forgiveness, and the willingness to resolve matters in a peaceful and respectful manner.

## Social Responsibility and Charity

Social responsibility and charity hold a significant place in the teachings of Islam, emphasizing the importance of compassion and generosity towards fellow human beings. Islamic principles emphasize the act of giving back to society and fulfilling one's duty towards those in need.

In Islam, the concept of social responsibility is deeply rooted in the belief that all individuals are responsible for the welfare of their community and society as a whole. Muslims are encouraged to be active participants in addressing social issues, alleviating poverty, and promoting the well-being of others. This commitment to social responsibility is seen as an essential part of living a righteous and fulfilling life.

Charity, known as "Zakat" in Islam, is one of the five pillars of the faith. It refers to the obligatory act of giving a portion of one's wealth to those less fortunate. This act is not merely regarded as a charitable deed, but a means of purifying one's wealth and seeking the pleasure of God. It is a reminder that material possessions are not an end in themselves, but rather a means to benefit others.

Zakat is an obligation for Muslims who possess a certain amount of wealth that reaches the "Nisab" (a specific threshold). This act of giving is not seen as a burden, but as a means of strengthening the bonds within society and eradicating poverty. It is also an opportunity for Muslims to express gratitude for the blessings they have received by sharing them with others in a responsible and dignified manner.

Charity in Islam extends beyond monetary contributions. Muslims are encouraged to engage in acts of voluntary charity, known as "Sadaqah," which can take various forms such as donating time, skills, or resources to uplift the disadvantaged or support beneficial causes. These acts of kindness and generosity are considered as integral components of a meaningful and compassionate life in Islam.

Islamic teachings emphasize the importance of being aware of the needs of others and responding to them with empathy and compassion. Islam promotes a culture that encourages individuals to seek out opportunities to make a positive difference in the lives of others, regardless of their religious, ethnic, or social backgrounds.

This inclusive approach exemplifies the universality of Islamic values of compassion, justice, and harmony.

## Inclusivity and Promoting Harmony

Inclusivity and promoting harmony are fundamental values within the Islamic faith, echoing the teachings and principles enshrined in the Quran. Islam encourages believers to embrace diversity and fosters an environment of acceptance, respect, and unity among its followers.

One of the core beliefs in Islam is the concept of ummah, which highlights the universal brotherhood and sisterhood of all Muslims. This principle emphasizes that regardless of race, ethnicity, nationality, or social status, all Muslims are considered equal and are united in their devotion to Allah.

Islamic teachings advocate for just and fair treatment of all individuals, irrespective of their background. The Quran states, "O mankind, indeed We have created you from male and female and made you peoples and tribes that you may know one another. Indeed, the most noble of you in the sight of Allah is the most righteous of you" (Quran, 49:13).

In Islamic history, notable examples demonstrate the promotion of inclusivity and harmony. For instance, during the time of the Prophet Muhammad, he established the Constitution of Medina, which granted equal rights and protection to all residents, regardless of their faith.

Moreover, Islam encourages Muslims to engage in dialogue and build bridges with people from different beliefs and backgrounds. The faith places great emphasis on compassion, kindness, and empathy towards others. Prophet Muhammad himself exemplified these qualities, regularly engaging with individuals of diverse backgrounds and treating them with utmost respect and fairness.

Promoting harmony within the Islamic community also involves actively combating discrimination and prejudice. The Quran condemns bigotry and prejudice, instructing Muslims to "stand firmly for justice, even if it is against yourselves, your parents, or your kin" (Quran, 4:135).

Islamic scholars and leaders have a significant role in promoting inclusivity and fostering harmony within the Muslim community. They emphasize the importance of understanding and implementing the core principles of Islam, focusing on the values of compassion, justice, and equality.

Efforts to promote inclusivity and harmony within Islam can be witnessed through various initiatives around the world. Mosques and Islamic centers often organize interfaith dialogues, cultural exchanges, and community outreach programs to build bridges and promote understanding between people of different beliefs. Muslims are encouraged to actively participate in such endeavors, fostering social cohesion and a sense of belonging for all.

CHAPTER 9

# Family Life in Islam

In the Islamic faith, the concept of family holds immense importance and is deeply valued. We briefly touched on the importance of family in our last chapter, but let's delve into this important subject in more detail.

Put simply, family is considered the cornerstone of society, rooted in mutual love, respect, and support that forms the building blocks of a harmonious and fulfilling life.

Islam places great emphasis on maintaining strong family ties and upholding the bonds between relatives. The Quran highlights the significance of family and outlines the responsibilities of each family member. It emphasizes the obligation to care for and protect one another, to show kindness, and to treat one's parents with utmost respect and gratitude. The Quran also emphasizes the importance of maintaining strong relationships with extended family members, such as grandparents, aunts, uncles, and cousins.

Islam recognizes that families are not limited to blood relations alone. It encourages the formation of strong bonds within the wider community, treating fellow Muslims as brothers and sisters. This unity fosters a sense of belonging, solidarity, and support, creating a network of extended family members who care deeply for one another.

By valuing and nurturing family ties, Islam seeks to create a society built on love, compassion, and collective responsibility. This emphasis on family helps to create a support system wherein individuals find emotional, physical, and spiritual well-being. It provides a safe and nurturing environment for the development of its members, ensuring that they grow up with a strong sense of identity, love, and security.

## Marriage, Parenting, and Family Dynamics

Marriage, parenting, and family dynamics hold significant importance in Islam, with teachings rooted in love, compassion, and the pursuit of harmony within the family unit. Islam places a strong emphasis on the sanctity of marriage, considering it a sacred bond that brings spiritual, emotional, and physical fulfillment to individuals.

In Islam, marriage is seen as a means to complete one's faith and lead a righteous life. It is a contract based on mutual consent and understanding between a man and a woman, with both partners committing to love, respect, and support each other. The Holy Quran encourages spouses to be each other's comfort, symbolizing protection, support, and companionship.

Within the framework of Islam, parenting is considered a noble and rewarding responsibility. Muslim parents are urged to raise their children with love, mercy, fairness, and guidance. They are encouraged to instill Islamic values and teachings through affectionate and patient parenting methods, fostering a strong connection between children and their Creator.

Family dynamics in Islam are built upon love, respect, and mutual cooperation. The Quran emphasizes kindness, compassion, and maintaining harmonious relationships with family members. Parents are considered a source of immense wisdom and guidance, deserving of honor and caring support from their children. Similarly, children are expected to uphold the values of obedience, kindness, and gratitude towards their parents.

Importantly, Islam recognizes that families come in various forms and may face unique challenges. Whether it be blended families, single-parent households, or extended family setups, Islam encourages unity, understanding, and flexibility within these dynamics. The emphasis lies not on the structure of the family, but rather on nurturing an environment of love, respect, and spiritual growth.

In Islamic teachings, open communication and dialogue are essential within families. Recognizing and appreciating each family member's individuality, strengths, and weaknesses fosters an atmosphere of acceptance and support. Islam recognizes that family life can sometimes present challenges, and it encourages patience, forgiveness, and empathy to overcome obstacles and build stronger bonds.

Furthermore, Islam places great importance on the concept of extended family and community support. Grandparents, aunts, uncles, and close relatives play a significant role in the upbringing of children, providing additional guidance, wisdom, and love.

## Gender Roles and Responsibilities in Islam

In Islam, gender roles and responsibilities are outlined with a sense of purpose and harmony. While it is often misunderstood, it is essential to approach this topic with an open mind and delve into the complexities of Islamic teachings.

Islam promotes the concept of equality between men and women, emphasizing their inherent value and importance in society. Both genders are considered equal in their essence as human beings, and are granted equal access to spiritual growth and salvation. However, it is crucial to recognize that equality does not mean identical roles or responsibilities.

One key principle of gender roles in Islam is the complementarity between men and women. Islam acknowledges and values the unique capabilities and strengths of each gender, recognizing that they may naturally excel in different domains. Men are encouraged to take on the role of the protector and provider for their families, while women are entrusted with the nurturing and care of their households. These prescribed roles are not meant to limit or confine individuals, but rather to create a harmonious balance within the family structure.

It is important to note that these roles are not rigidly enforced, and Islam encourages flexibility according to individual circumstances and abilities. A woman, for instance, has the right to work and pursue an education outside of her household, if she so desires. Similarly, a man may take on household responsibilities and actively support his wife's career aspirations.

Islam recognizes the inherent dignity, rights, and potential of both genders, and encourages mutual respect and cooperation. It emphasizes the importance of consultation and shared decision-making within the family, ensuring that both perspectives are taken into account. Islam also emphasizes the value of kindness and compassion, reminding individuals to treat one another with fairness, love, and respect.

It is crucial to remember that gender roles and responsibilities within Islam should not be simplistically confined to traditional stereotypes or misconceptions. Islamic teachings promote a holistic approach to gender, embracing the unique qualities and potentials of men and women, while fostering an atmosphere of cooperation and mutual support within the family and society.

Overall, Islam embraces the concept of equality between men and women, while recognizing and appreciating their distinct nature and strengths. The prescribed gender roles and responsibilities in Islam are designed to create a harmonious balance within the family structure, ensuring the well-being and happiness of all its members. It is through understanding, respect, and open-mindedness that we can appreciate the depth and wisdom behind these teachings, fostering a more inclusive and equitable society for all.

## Respecting Elders

Respecting elders plays a significant role in nurturing a harmonious and compassionate society. It is not merely a matter of etiquette, but rather a moral obligation that holds immense importance. The teachings of Islam emphasize the utmost honor and reverence that should be given to elders, highlighting their wisdom, experience, and the blessings they bring to our lives.

Respecting elders is deeply rooted in the teachings of the Quran, which urges believers to uphold this virtue. Allah, in His infinite wisdom, recognizes the inherent wisdom and guidance that comes with age, and thus commands us to treat our elders with utmost respect and kindness. Islam teaches that honoring and serving one's parents and the elderly is a means of attaining the pleasure of Allah. In the Quran, it is stated, "Your Lord has decreed that you worship none but Him, and that you be kind to your parents. Whether one or both of them attain old age in your lifetime, say not to them a word of contempt, nor repel them, but address them in terms of honor" (Quran, 17:23).

This profound respect for elders is further reinforced by the Sunnah of the Prophet Muhammad, who exemplified this virtue in his interactions with older members of society. The Prophet Muhammad consistently demonstrated patience, compassion, and empathy towards the elderly, acknowledging their worth and seeking their guidance. He emphasized that those who honor and respect their elders will be blessed with longevity and divine mercy.

In Islam, respecting elders encompasses a wide range of actions. It goes beyond simply addressing them with honorific titles or granting them precedence in social gatherings. It involves actively listening to their stories, valuing their experiences, seeking their advice, and assisting them in their daily tasks. Islam teaches that serving the elderly is a means of purifying one's soul, and it brings numerous blessings and rewards from Allah.

It is crucial to recognize that honoring elders extends not only to our biological parents and direct relatives, but to all elderly individuals, regardless of their background or social status. Islam encourages us to demonstrate kindness, patience, and compassion towards seniors in our communities. This could involve visiting nursing homes, volunteering to assist with their needs, or simply showing sincere concern for their well-being.

Moreover, Islam considers the duty of respecting elders as an opportunity to attain immense blessings and rewards. By demonstrating honor towards the elderly, we not only fulfill our obligations as Muslims, but we also contribute to the cohesion and harmony of the entire society.

## Chapter 10

# Islamic Holidays and Festivals

Throughout the Islamic calendar year, believers around the world gather to commemorate significant milestones in their faith, joyfully embracing their traditions and expressing heartfelt gratitude to the divine. It is within these celebrations that the Islamic community comes together, fostering unity, spirituality, and a deeper connection with each other and with the divine presence.

These holy occasions are deeply rooted in centuries-old traditions and hold great significance for Muslims across the globe. Each festival bears a unique narrative, conveying essential moral values and lessons that resonate with the core principles of Islam. Let's explore the major Islamic holidays and festivals in more detail. It's important to note that Islamic holidays follow the lunar Islamic calendar, so the dates and celebrations may vary each year in relation to the Gregorian calendar.

## Ramadan

Ramadan, deriving its name from the Arabic word "ramad," which means scorching heat, is the ninth month of the Islamic lunar calendar. It holds great significance for Muslims worldwide, serving as a time of devotion, reflection, and spiritual growth.

During Ramadan, Muslims abstain from consuming food, water, and other physical necessities from dawn until sunset. This act of fasting is a pillar of Islam and is observed as a means of purifying the soul, increasing self-discipline, and empathizing with those who suffer from hunger and thirst on a regular basis.

The pre-dawn meal, known as Suhoor, is taken before the break of dawn, providing nourishment and energy to sustain Muslims throughout the day of fasting. At sunset, families and communities come together to break their fast in a practice called Iftar. This moment is cherished as a communal gathering, often marked with dates, water, and other traditional foods, followed by prayers and the recitation of the Holy Quran.

Ramadan also encourages acts of charity and generosity. Many Muslims engage in giving to the less fortunate, sharing their blessings with those in need. It is believed that such acts of compassion hold immense reward during this blessed month.

In addition to fasting and charitable deeds, Muslims engage in heightened spiritual practices during Ramadan. They spend extra time in prayer, seeking to deepen their connection with Allah and seeking forgiveness for their past sins. Nightly prayers, called Taraweeh, are performed in congregation at mosques, with the recitation of the entire Quran spread over the course of the month.

Laylat al-Qadr, also known as the Night of Power, is regarded as the most important night during Ramadan. Muslims believe that on this special night, the first verses of the Quran were revealed to Prophet Muhammad. It is a night of intense worship and reflection, considered to be better than a thousand months.

Throughout Ramadan, Muslims strive to cleanse their thoughts, words, and actions, aiming to achieve spiritual rejuvenation and a strengthened bond with their faith. The month serves as a reminder of self-discipline, empathy, and gratitude, while fostering a sense of unity, compassion, and a deeper connection with Allah.

Ramadan is a time of great importance, where Muslims around the world come together to observe fasting, offer prayers, engage in acts of charity, and seek spiritual growth. It is a period that encourages self-reflection, growth, and devotion, reminding individuals of the core values of their faith.

## Eid al-Fitr

Eid al-Fitr, often referred to as the Festival of Breaking the Fast, is one of the most significant religious observances for Muslims worldwide. It marks the end of the month-long fasting period of Ramadan, during which devout Muslims engage in dawn-to-dusk fasting, prayer, and acts of charity. This joyous occasion holds immense cultural and religious significance, celebrated with great enthusiasm and unity among the Muslim community.

The essence of Eid al-Fitr lies in the spirit of gratitude, generosity, and compassion. It serves as a time for Muslims to express their appreciation for the blessings bestowed upon them and to share their joys with family, friends, and those in need. As the new moon is sighted, signaling the end of Ramadan, families fervently prepare for the festivities that await them.

On the day of Eid, Muslims dress in their finest attire to attend special congregational prayers known as Salat al-Eid. These prayers are held either in large open spaces, mosques, or community centers, where individuals come together to listen to sermons and partake in communal worship. The prayer is followed by a sermon, which emphasizes unity, forgiveness, and the importance of maintaining good relations with others.

After the prayers, households often gather for a lavish breakfast, known as "Eid al-Fitr feast." Family and friends exchange warm greetings of "Eid Mubarak" while enjoying delectable traditional delicacies. Sweet treats, such as sheer khurma (vermicelli pudding) and baklava, are shared abundantly, symbolizing the sweetness and joy of the occasion.

Furthermore, Eid al-Fitr is a time of giving. It is customary for Muslims to provide financial assistance, known as "Zakat al-Fitr," to the less fortunate before the day of Eid. This mandatory act of charity ensures that everyone can partake in the celebrations and experience the happiness that the festival brings. Many also take this opportunity to visit and distribute gifts to family, friends, and neighbors, fostering a sense of community and reinforcing bonds of love and companionship.

Throughout the day, families engage in various social activities, such as visiting loved ones, hosting and attending feasts, exchanging gifts, and engaging in lively conversations. Children, in particular, eagerly anticipate receiving "Eidi," monetary gifts given by elders as a symbol of love and goodwill.

Eid al-Fitr not only serves as a time for celebration and merriment but also provides a chance for Muslims to reflect on their spiritual journey during Ramadan and renew their commitment to personal growth and benevolence. Additionally, the festive atmosphere encourages social harmony, as people from diverse backgrounds come together, embracing cultural diversity and promoting unity.

## Eid al-Adha

Eid al-Adha, also known as the Festival of Sacrifice, holds great significance in the Islamic faith. This joyous celebration commemorates the story of the Prophet Ibrahim's willingness to sacrifice his son as an act of obedience to God, who ultimately replaced his son with a ram as the sacrifice. Eid al-Adha serves as a reminder of the importance of faith, devotion, and selflessness.

The traditions and practices surrounding Eid al-Adha vary among different cultures, but there are several key elements that unite Muslims worldwide during this auspicious time. One central component is the act of sacrifice, where families who are able to do so prepare an animal, often a sheep or goat, to be sacrificed. This act symbolizes the willingness to sacrifice for the sake of God and to share blessings with those in need.

Prior to the sacrifice, Muslims gather for communal prayers at the mosque or an outdoor prayer ground. This special congregational prayer, known as Salat al-Eid, is performed as a way to express unity among the community and to seek blessings from God. It is a beautiful sight to witness people of all ages and backgrounds coming together in a collective display of devotion.

After completing the prayers, families and friends come together to exchange warm greetings and well wishes. It is customary to dress in new or clean clothes, signifying a fresh start and a renewed sense of spirituality. Giving gifts, especially to children, is also common during this time, enhancing the festive atmosphere and spreading joy among loved ones.

The real essence of Eid al-Adha lies in the spirit of generosity and charity. It is considered a time to share blessings with others, particularly the less fortunate. Many Muslims give a portion of the sacrificed animal's meat to those in need, ensuring that everyone can enjoy the festive meal. This act of philanthropy captures the true essence of Eid al-Adha, emphasizing the importance of compassion and solidarity.

Furthermore, gathering with family and loved ones is an integral part of the celebrations. People come together to share delicious meals, exchange stories, and strengthen their bonds. It is a time to appreciate and cherish the presence of loved ones, as well as to reflect on the blessings and mercies bestowed upon them.

Eid al-Adha is not only a time for celebration but also for self-reflection and spiritual growth. Muslims take this occasion to examine their personal sacrifices and strive towards becoming better individuals. It is a reminder to live a life dedicated to righteousness, compassion, and gratitude.

## Mawlid al-Nabi

Mawlid al-Nabi, also known as the Prophet's Birthday or Milad un-Nabi, is an important observance in the Islamic faith. It commemorates the birth of the Prophet Muhammad, the founder of Islam, and is celebrated with great reverence and joy by Muslims around the world.

Mawlid al-Nabi holds significant cultural and religious significance and is usually observed on the 12th day of Rabi' al-Awwal, the third month of the Islamic lunar calendar. It is a time to honor and reflect upon the life, teachings, and example of the Prophet Muhammad.

During this auspicious occasion, Muslims engage in various traditions and practices. These customs may vary depending on cultural and regional differences. However, some common observances are prevalent among believers.

Mosques and Islamic centers are often adorned with colorful decorations and lights, creating a festive atmosphere that signifies the joyous nature of the celebration. Muslims gather to offer special prayers, known as "Naat" or "Mawlid" gatherings, where they recite poetry, hymns, and praise the Prophet Muhammad. These gatherings provide a space for communal reflection, remembrance, and gratitude towards the Prophet's teachings.

Recitation of the Holy Quran and stories about the life of the Prophet Muhammad are frequently shared during Mawlid al-Nabi. It serves as an opportunity to educate individuals, particularly the younger generation, about the significance and lessons derived from the Prophet's life and his teachings of compassion, justice, and humility.

Charitable acts and giving are emphasized during this time as well. Muslims often engage in acts of generosity, such as giving alms or providing food to those in need. This embodies the spirit of benevolence propagated by the Prophet Muhammad and serves as a reminder of the importance of serving humanity.

Another notable tradition associated with Mawlid al-Nabi is the procession or parade, known as a "Milad." These processions are characterized by participants chanting religious hymns, offering prayers, and holding banners or flags. They serve as a public expression of devotion and admiration for the Prophet Muhammad.

In addition to these practices, families typically come together to share meals, exchange gifts, and engage in acts of kindness towards one another. It is a time for strengthening bonds of kinship and fostering a sense of unity and love within the community.

Mawlid al-Nabi offers Muslims an occasion to celebrate and honor the birth of the Prophet Muhammad, while also reflecting on his teachings and embodying his noble character. It is a time of joy, remembrance, and gratitude, as believers strive to emulate the Prophet's ideals and values in their daily lives.

## Laylat al-Qadr

Laylat al-Qadr, also known as the Night of Power, holds great significance for Muslims around the world. This auspicious night falls during the holy month of Ramadan, and it is believed to be the night when the first verses of the Quran were revealed to Prophet Muhammad.

Laylat al-Qadr holds immense spiritual importance, as it is considered to be better than a thousand months' worth of worship. Many Muslims spend this night engaged in prayer, reciting the Quran, and seeking forgiveness for their sins. It is believed that any act of worship performed on this night carries immense blessings.

The exact date of Laylat al-Qadr is not known, as it is hidden within the last ten nights of Ramadan. However, the odd nights of the last ten nights, such as the 21st, 23rd, 25th, 27th, or 29th night, are commonly observed as potential nights of great significance.

Muslims devote themselves to various traditions and practices on Laylat al-Qadr. Many spend the entire night in intense prayer and reflection, seeking closeness to Allah and striving for spiritual purification. Mosques and homes are often illuminated with lights, and people gather together in congregational prayers.

Reciting the Quran is highly encouraged during this night, with Muslims often engaging in recitation to seek a deeper connection with the words of Allah. Charity is also practiced abundantly, with believers eager to contribute to the welfare of others and increase their chances of attaining blessings and forgiveness.

Additionally, it is customary for Muslims to engage in supplication, beseeching Allah for guidance, blessings, forgiveness, and mercy. It is believed that any sincere prayer during this blessed night has a higher chance of being answered.

Moreover, some Muslims adhere to the practice of itikaf, which involves seclusion in a mosque for the last 10 nights of Ramadan, specifically with the intention of seeking Laylat al-Qadr. During this period, individuals disconnect themselves from worldly distractions and dedicate their time to prayer, remembrance of Allah, and self-reflection.

Laylat al-Qadr is a night of inner peace, spiritual rejuvenation, and an opportunity for believers to enhance their relationship with Allah. By partaking in the various traditions and practices associated with this night, Muslims seek to reap the benefits of this profound occasion, aiming to purify their souls, seek forgiveness, and draw nearer to their Creator.

## Ashura

Ashura is a significant observance in the Islamic calendar, widely commemorated by Muslims worldwide. Derived from the Arabic word for "tenth," this annual event falls on the 10th day of

Muharram, the first month of the Islamic lunar calendar. Ashura holds both historical and spiritual significance, marking different events for various Muslim communities.

One of the notable events remembered during Ashura is the rescue of the Prophet Moses, known as Musa in Arabic, and the Israelites from the clutches of Pharaoh in ancient Egypt. As mentioned in the Quran, it is believed that Allah parted the Red Sea, allowing Moses and his followers to escape the wrath of Pharaoh's army. This miraculous event is an emblem of divine intervention and triumph over oppression.

For Shia Muslims, Ashura is a profoundly poignant occasion, reminding them of the martyrdom of Imam Hussein, the grandson of the Prophet Muhammad, in the 7th century. This tragic event occurred during the Battle of Karbala, where Imam Hussein and his small group of supporters valiantly stood against a much larger army. The courageous sacrifice of Imam Hussein and his companions is seen as a symbol of unwavering faith, justice, and standing up against tyranny.

During Ashura, Shia Muslims engage in a range of practices to honor the memory of Imam Hussein. These may include mourning processions where participants dress in black attire and march through streets, reciting elegies and hymns to express their grief and solidarity. In some communities, theatrical reenactments known as "ta'ziyah" are performed, depicting the tragic events of Karbala to evoke empathy and emotional connection.

An aspect of Ashura considered commendable by Muslims across various sects is fasting. Many believers observe a voluntary fast on the ninth and tenth days of Muharram, emulating the Prophet Muhammad's recommended practice. This fast is not obligatory, but those who choose to observe it do so to express gratitude, seek spiritual purification, and reflect on the significance of sacrifice and resilience.

In addition to fasting, acts of charity, compassion, and kindness are encouraged during Ashura. Muslims often participate in distributing food and drinks to the less fortunate, emphasizing the values of generosity and communal unity. This day serves as a reminder to extend a helping hand to those in need and make a positive impact in society.

It is important to note that Ashura holds different meanings and practices depending on individual beliefs and cultural customs. Muslims observe this occasion with reverence, reflecting on the historical events and drawing inspiration from the values of faith, courage, and selflessness exemplified within them.

## Chapter 11

# Islamic Art, Architecture, and Culture

Islamic art and architecture encompass a tradition that spans both time and geography. From the dazzling palaces of Moorish Spain to the intricate patterns of Persian carpets, Islamic art has evolved and flourished over centuries, leaving an indelible mark on the world.

Rooted in the tenets of the Islamic faith, this art form represents not only an aesthetic expression but also a cultural and spiritual connection. In this chapter, we will explore the diverse facets of Islamic art and architecture, highlighting their underlying principles, historical development, and unique characteristics.

The roots of Islamic art can be traced back to the 7th century CE, concurrent with the rise of the Islamic faith. Following the death of the Prophet Muhammad, Islamic civilization began to flourish, encompassing various regions from the Arabian Peninsula to North Africa, Persia, and beyond. As Islamic territories expanded, so too did the intermingling of cultural influences, resulting in a rich and diverse artistic legacy.

## Characteristics of Islamic Art

Islamic art is characterized by a distinct visual language that marries geometry, abstract patterns, and nature-inspired motifs. An aversion to figurative representation stems from the belief in aniconism, which discourages the depiction of human and animal forms. This prohibition led to the development of a unique style that relies heavily on calligraphy, arabesque designs, and tessellation.

Arabesque designs, often found adorning surfaces, reflect the intertwining forms reminiscent of foliage and plants. These intricate patterns symbolize the unity of nature under the dominion of a higher power. The exquisite repetition and interplay of shapes and lines in Islamic art mesmerize the viewer, evoking a feeling of harmony and transcendence.

Geometry constitutes a fundamental element of Islamic art and architecture. Elaborate mathematical principles guide the rigorous construction of monuments and decorative motifs. The notion of unity and divine order is mirrored in the precise geometric patterns seen in domes, arches, and tilework. From the symmetrical compositions of the hypostyle prayer halls to the intricate lattice screens of the mihrab, geometry reigns supreme, invoking a sense of balance and serenity.

**Materials and Techniques**

Islamic art employs a wide variety of materials and techniques, reflecting the ingenuity and craftsmanship of its artisans. Intricate calligraphy, ceramic tilework, and exquisite wood and metal craftsmanship are just a few examples of the diverse mediums utilized.

Ceramic tilework, known as zellij, adorns palaces, mosques, and urban architecture throughout the Islamic world. These vibrant, geometrically patterned tiles create visually striking surfaces that dazzle with a kaleidoscope of colors. The meticulous cutting, glazing, and firing involved in their production attest to the level of skill and attention to detail possessed by the artisans.

## Architectural Marvels

Islamic architecture is renowned for its monumental structures and breathtaking beauty. Mosques, madrasas (religious schools), palaces, and mausoleums serve as showcases for both artistic expression and spiritual devotion.

Perhaps the most famous example of Islamic architecture is the magnificent Alhambra in Granada, Spain. This UNESCO World Heritage site embodies the fusion of Islamic and Andalusian art, boasting intricately carved stucco, stunning courtyards, and tranquil gardens. The Alhambra stands as a testament to the harmonious blending of artistic elements found within Islamic architecture.

Islamic art and architecture provide a captivating glimpse into the rich cultural heritage of the Islamic world. Rooted in the principles of the Islamic faith, this art form showcases a profound devotion to both the divine and the pursuit of beauty. A celebration of geometry, intricate patterns, and exquisite craftsmanship, Islamic art has left an indelible mark on the artistic and architectural landscape of the world. Through its timeless allure, Islamic art continues to inspire and captivate audiences, fostering a deeper understanding and appreciation of the interconnectedness of diverse cultures.

## Calligraphy & Decorative Motifs

Islamic calligraphy and decorative motifs are integral components of Islamic art, embodying the essence of Islamic culture and spirituality. With its origins deeply rooted in the early centuries of Islam, these artistic expressions display a mature and profound beauty that transcends time and borders.

Calligraphy, the art of beautiful writing, holds a cherished position in Islamic culture. It emerged as a form of artistic expression due to the veneration of the written word in the Islamic tradition. Islamic calligraphy can be traced back to the time of the Prophet

Muhammad, who himself emphasized the importance of writing in various aspects of life, including religious scripts and poetry. Over time, calligraphy became a symbol of divine revelation and an embodiment of the divine word of God.

One of the most distinctive features of Islamic calligraphy is the importance given to the Quran, the holy book of Islam. The reverence for the Quran led calligraphers to dedicate their skills to the oldest form of Islamic calligraphy—Kufic script. Kufic, with its angular and bold lettering, was widely employed to write the Quran and decorate Islamic monuments during the early Islamic period. It conveys a sense of strength and stability, reflecting the enduring nature of the Islamic faith.

As Islam spread across different regions, calligraphy evolved, leading to the development of various script styles. One of the most revered styles is Naskh, characterized by its flowing and rounded letters. Naskh became the dominant script not only for writing religious texts but also for everyday writing and official documents. Its harmony of proportions and legibility contributed to its widespread use and popularity. Nastaliq, a later development, is defined by its elongated and fluid strokes, lending it an elegant and graceful quality. This style became especially prominent in Persian and Urdu calligraphy.

Islamic calligraphy often intertwines with decoration, weaving intricate patterns and motifs into the written word. These decorative elements evolved alongside calligraphy, showcasing a stunning creativity and skill. The motifs commonly used include geometric patterns, arabesques, and floral designs.

Geometric patterns, with their precision and symmetry, are hallmarks of Islamic art. Stars, triangles, hexagons, and circles are combined in intricate arrangements, forming mesmerizing designs that seem to expand into infinity. These geometric motifs symbolize the underlying order and harmony in the universe, reflecting the Islamic belief in the unity and perfection of God's creation.

Arabesques, characterized by their fluid and curvilinear nature, are another significant decorative feature. These intricate and interlocking vine-like patterns, often intertwined with calligraphy, convey a sense of movement and dynamism. Arabesques serve as a reminder of the divine energy flowing through the world and represent the interconnection between the spiritual and physical realms.

Floral designs in Islamic art draw inspiration from nature's beauty. Flowers, leaves, and vines are meticulously depicted in a stylized manner, reflecting an idealized perception of the natural world. These motifs symbolize growth, renewal, and the cycle of life, reminding viewers of God's bountiful creation.

Islamic calligraphy and decorative motifs are not limited to religious contexts alone. They adorn a multitude of objects, including ceramics, textiles, architecture, and manuscripts. From the grandeur of mosque interiors to the elegance of everyday objects, calligraphy and decorative motifs serve as a constant reminder of the beauty and spirituality inherent in Islamic art.

## Notable Examples of Islamic Art & Architecture Worldwide

Islamic art and architecture have left an indelible mark on the world, with a multitude of magnificent creations that reflect the rich cultural heritage and astonishing craftsmanship of the Muslim world. From intricate geometric patterns to breathtaking mosques, here are 10 notable examples of Islamic art and architecture that have captivated admirers worldwide.

- **Dome of the Rock, Jerusalem**: This iconic structure, built in the 7th century, showcases stunning early Islamic architecture. Adorned with intricate tile work, calligraphy, and colorful mosaics, the golden dome stands as an architectural masterpiece.

- **Alhambra, Granada, Spain:** A testament to the Islamic presence in medieval Europe, the Alhambra is a splendid fortress palace that showcases the Nasrid dynasty's decorative prowess. Its captivating beauty lies in its intricate tile work, ornate arches, tranquil courtyards, and serene gardens.

- **Sheikh Zayed Mosque, Abu Dhabi, UAE:** Among the modern wonders of Islamic architecture, this awe-inspiring mosque stands tall. With its pristine white façade, intricate carvings, and magnificent domes, it beautifully blends traditional and contemporary elements.

- **Topkapi Palace, Istanbul, Turkey:** Once the residence of Ottoman sultans, this sprawling palace complex is a masterpiece of Islamic art and architecture. The opulent courtyards, intricate tile work, and stunning views of the Bosphorus make it a must-visit destination.

- **Great Mosque of Cordoba, Cordoba, Spain:** Witness the magnificence of early Islamic art at this architectural gem. Its iconic red and white striped arches, meticulously intricate mosaics, and serene courtyard exude a harmonious blend of Islamic and Christian influences.

- **Sultan Omar Ali Saifuddien Mosque, Bandar Seri Begawan, Brunei:** This architectural marvel stands as a symbol of modern Islamic design. Its shimmering golden dome, meticulous marble detailing, and serene surroundings make it a sight to behold.

- **Taj Mahal, Agra, India:** Regarded as one of the wonders of the world, the Taj Mahal is an epitome of Islamic architecture's grandeur. A mausoleum built by Emperor Shah Jahan for his beloved wife, it harmoniously blends Persian, Indian, and Islamic styles.

- **Great Mosque of Samarra, Samarra, Iraq:** Known for its towering minaret, this ancient mosque is one of the largest in the world. Its unique spiral architecture and mesmerizing stucco designs make it an exceptional example of early Islamic art.

- **Nasir ol Molk Mosque, Shiraz, Iran:** This enchanting mosque is renowned for its captivating stained glass windows that cast a kaleidoscope of colors during sunrise. The intricate tile work and delicate mirror mosaics add a touch of magic to its ethereal ambiance.

- **The Blue Mosque (Sultan Ahmed Mosque), Istanbul, Turkey:** A true jewel of Ottoman architecture, this famous mosque astounds visitors with its six towering minarets, vibrant blue tiles, and cascading domes. Its grandeur is further complemented by the stunning interior adorned with intricate calligraphy and Iznik tile work.

These 10 examples represent just a fraction of the remarkable Islamic art and architecture found worldwide. Each structure possesses its own unique charm and significance, showcasing the incredible talent, creativity, and devotion that has shaped the Islamic artistic legacy.

## Chapter 12

# Islam & Other Religions

Islam offers a distinct perspective on religious pluralism. Rooted in the belief of the oneness of God and the finality of the prophethood of Muhammad, Islam acknowledges the existence of multiple religions while maintaining its own unique understanding of truth and spirituality. In the contemporary world, where diverse religious beliefs coexist, Islam emphasizes peaceful coexistence and dialogue with adherents of other faiths.

At the core of Islam's perspective on religious pluralism lies the Quranic concept of "Ummatan Wasatan" or the "Middle Nation." Islam considers itself to be the balanced and moderate path between the extremes of exclusivism and relativism. It encourages its adherents to engage in a respectful and compassionate manner with people of different faiths.

One of the fundamental teachings of Islam is the concept of "Tawhid," the belief in the oneness of God. Islam considers itself as the continuation of the monotheistic traditions that came before it, such as Judaism and Christianity, while also embracing the uniqueness of its own message. Muslims are enjoined to proclaim the unity of God and invite others to monotheism, but they are also commanded to treat people of other faiths with kindness and fairness.

The Quran acknowledges the existence of different religions and recognizes the diversity of human beliefs. It states, "For each of you, We have appointed a law and a way. And if Allah had willed, He could have made you one nation. But that He may test you in what

He has given you" (Quran, 5:48). This verse highlights that religious diversity is part of Allah's divine wisdom and a test for humanity.

Additionally, Islam places great importance on the concept of religious freedom. The Quran states, "There shall be no compulsion in the matters of religion" (Quran, 2:256). This verse underscores the principle that no one should be forced to embrace Islam or any other religion against their will. Islam respects the autonomy of individuals to choose their own beliefs, recognizing that faith can only be truly meaningful when it is a matter of personal conviction.

Islam also emphasizes the necessity of peaceful coexistence and mutual respect among people of different faiths. According to Islamic teachings, believers are urged to engage in dialogue with adherents of other religions in a respectful manner, seeking common ground and promoting harmony. The Quran enshrines this principle by stating, "Say, 'O disbelievers, I do not worship what you worship. Nor are you worshippers of what I worship. Nor will I be a worshipper of what you worship. Nor will you be worshippers of what I worship. For you is your religion, and for me is my religion'" (Quran, 109:1-6).

Islamic history provides examples of religious pluralism being embraced and protected. During the rule of Prophet Muhammad, he entered into agreements with various religious communities, such as the Covenant of Medina, guaranteeing their rights and freedom of worship. Similarly, the Ottoman Empire, a Muslim-majority state, followed a policy of tolerance towards its non-Muslim subjects, allowing them to practice their own faiths and establishing a system of coexistence known as "Millet."

Nevertheless, it is important to acknowledge that interpretations of Islamic teachings vary among scholars and individuals. Some Muslims may have more exclusivist views, viewing Islam as the only true religion, while others may adopt a more inclusive and pluralistic stance. However, the overall message of Islam encourages respecting the rights of individuals to hold differing beliefs and fostering peaceful relations with people of other faiths.

## Interfaith Dialogue & Cooperation

Islam portrays a profound commitment to fostering understanding, promoting unity, and embracing harmonious coexistence among diverse communities. Embedded within its teachings are the principles and values that encourage Muslims to engage in meaningful conversations, build bridges, and seek common ground with people of different faiths.

Islam firmly establishes the significance of peaceful coexistence and respect for the beliefs and practices of others. With a strong emphasis on social justice, compassion, and empathy, Muslims are encouraged to nurture connections with people from various faith traditions, fostering bonds based on mutual understanding and respect.

The Quran encourages Muslims to interact with others in a manner that is characterized by wisdom, clarity, and utmost kindness.

Islamic intellectual tradition actively engages in interfaith dialogue, as scholars seek to foster an atmosphere of understanding and cooperation. Deeply rooted in the Quranic teachings of respecting diversity, scholars contribute to academic discussions and theological dialogues aimed at bridging differences and promoting peaceful coexistence. Their writings and discourses serve as a source of inspiration, guiding Muslims towards embracing pluralism and recognizing the value of experiencing and learning from diverse perspectives.

Furthermore, the concept of interfaith dialogue within Islam extends beyond mere tolerance. It encourages a deeper appreciation of shared values and shared humanity, while also recognizing and respecting religious differences. This acknowledgement of diversity is not seen as a challenge or threat, but rather as an opportunity for personal growth, societal enrichment, and a source of collective wisdom.

Engaging in interfaith dialogue and cooperation allows Muslims to challenge stereotypes, dispel misunderstandings, and build enduring relationships. Through meaningful conversations, Muslims can address misconceptions and clarify any doubts, while also promoting an authentic understanding of Islam's teachings. By focusing on shared values and common goals, Muslims can work together with people from different faiths to address pressing issues such as poverty, injustice, and environmental sustainability.

## Commonalities & Differences Between Islam and Other Faiths

Religion has been and continues to be an integral part of human societies, providing individuals with a sense of purpose, guidance, and moral framework. As one of the major world religions, Islam shares some commonalities with other faiths while also exhibiting certain distinct characteristics. This section aims to explore the commonalities and differences between Islam and other religions, fostering understanding and promoting interfaith dialogue.

### Commonalities

Despite their unique beliefs and practices, religions often share common foundational elements that emphasize values such as love, compassion, and respect for others. Islam is no exception in this regard. For instance, Islam shares a belief in monotheism with other Abrahamic religions such as Christianity and Judaism. Muslims, Christians, and Jews all worship and acknowledge the existence of a single, supreme deity.

Moreover, most religions uphold some form of moral values and ethical teachings. Islam, for example, places great emphasis on virtuous behavior, including honesty, humility, justice, and generosity. This emphasis on moral conduct and virtue is also found in other religions. Buddhism, for instance, advocates for concepts such as compassion and non-violence, while Hinduism promotes righteousness and the pursuit of self-realization.

Additionally, religions often promote communal practices that foster a sense of togetherness and belonging. Islam, like Christianity and Judaism, encourages communal prayer and gatherings. This practice not only helps establish a connection with a higher power but also promotes unity among believers. Similarly, Hinduism encourages congregational prayers and rituals, while Buddhism places significant importance on collective meditation and chanting.

## Differences

While religion serves as a unifying force, it is also important to recognize the unique aspects that set various faiths apart. In the case of Islam, several key differences distinguish it from other religions.

One distinctive feature of Islam is the concept of the prophethood of Muhammad. With Muhammad viewed as the final prophet, Islam presents a break from the traditional prophetic lineages found in Christianity, which recognizes Jesus Christ as the central figure, and Judaism, which venerates Moses and other prophets. The centrality of Muhammad to Islam has influenced its theology and practices, such as the pillars of Islam and the reverence given to the Quran.

Another notable difference lies in the rituals and observances that define each particular faith. In Islam, the Five Pillars form the core obligations of a Muslim's life. Conversely, Christianity centers on concepts such as faith in Jesus as the savior, baptism, and partaking in the Eucharist. Hinduism, being a vast and diverse religion, encompasses numerous rituals, beliefs, and practices catering to individual preferences and regional traditions.

The scriptures or holy texts of various religions also vary significantly. Islam holds the Quran as its sacred text, believed to be the literal word of God. In contrast, Christianity draws primarily from the Old and New Testaments of the Bible, containing teachings, histories, and parables. Hinduism possesses a large body of texts, including the Vedas, Upanishads, Ramayana, Mahabharata, and Bhagavad Gita, providing a comprehensive framework for spiritual life and moral conduct.

While examining the commonalities and differences between Islam and other religions, one can appreciate the diversity and richness of human spiritual experiences. Although there are distinctive aspects that make each faith unique, there are also shared values and teachings that bind them together. By fostering an open and respectful dialogue, individuals can deepen their understanding of various religions, leading to greater harmony and acceptance in our global society.

# Chapter 13

# Islam in the Modern World

The Muslim community, as one of the world's largest and most diverse religious groups, faces a multitude of challenges and opportunities in the contemporary world. These challenges range from socio-political issues such as Islamophobia and discrimination to internal struggles stemming from differing interpretations of Islamic teachings.

Nonetheless, Muslims today also encounter promising opportunities for positive change, empowerment, and the promotion of peace and understanding. This essay will explore some of the significant challenges and potential avenues for progress that Muslims are navigating in their daily lives.

## Challenges

### Islamophobia and Discrimination

One of the greatest challenges facing Muslims today is the rise of Islamophobia and its various manifestations globally. Prejudice and discrimination against Muslims, fueled by ignorance and media narratives portraying Islam negatively, have led to marginalization, hate crimes, and exclusion. Countering this bigotry necessitates education, interfaith dialogue, and changing narratives to foster greater understanding and inclusivity.

### Radicalization and Extremism

While a negligible fraction of Muslims worldwide espouse extremist ideologies, the actions of a few have unfairly tarnished the image of the entire community. Combating radicalization necessitates an integrated approach combining effective counter-terrorism strategies with a focus on education, economic opportunities, and social empowerment. Addressing the root causes of radicalization, such as socio-economic disparities and political grievances, is crucial for long-term solutions.

### Internal Struggles and Fragmentation

Muslims today exhibit a diverse range of interpretations and practices, leading to internal divisions and fragmentation within the community. Disagreements on theological matters, cultural influences, and socio-political perspectives can often hinder unity and collective efforts. Recognizing and celebrating this diversity while fostering a spirit of tolerance, mutual respect, and understanding is vital for promoting a harmonious and inclusive Muslim community.

## Opportunities

### Empowerment of Muslim Women

In recent years, there has been a noticeable shift toward empowering Muslim women in both religious and secular spheres. Women are increasingly playing active roles as religious scholars, educators, and community leaders. This empowerment is crucial in challenging misconceptions and stereotypes while creating opportunities for Muslim women to contribute their unique perspectives to various fields.

Encouraging gender equality and ensuring access to education and employment opportunities further fuels the advancement of Muslim women, benefitting society as a whole.

## Technological Advancements and Digital Connectivity

Muslims today have unparalleled opportunities for global digital connectivity, enabling them to shape narratives, debunk stereotypes, and build constructive dialogues with people of different faiths and cultural backgrounds.

Social media platforms, podcasts, and blogs provide platforms for Muslims to share their stories, dispel myths, and advocate for peace, justice, and coexistence. Leveraging these digital tools enables Muslims to forge new alliances, establish networks, and create spaces for dialogue within and beyond their communities.

Interfaith Dialogue and Collaborative Efforts

In the face of growing tensions and divisions between religious groups, interfaith dialogue offers an avenue for Muslims to engage constructively with individuals from different faith traditions. By fostering understanding, cooperation, and shared values, interfaith initiatives can bridge divides, break down stereotypes, and promote peaceful coexistence. Joint efforts to address global challenges such as climate change, poverty, and conflict can also create opportunities for mutual learning and collaboration across religious boundaries.

Muslims across the globe face a complex array of challenges, ranging from prejudice and discrimination to internal divisions. However, amidst these hurdles, numerous opportunities have emerged for positive change and growth. By embracing these opportunities, Muslims can be at the forefront of fostering harmonious societies, promoting social justice, and championing coexistence in an ever-changing world.

## Islamophobia, Extremism, & Misconceptions

We've briefly mentioned Islamophobia and extremism as challenges for Muslims in the modern day, but these are extremely important subjects which require more reflection. There are countless misconceptions about the Muslim faith, and breaking down these incorrect views is vital to ensure a peaceful and inclusive society.

**Understanding Islamophobia**

Muslims have faced prejudice and discrimination for centuries, but the term "Islamophobia" gained prominence in recent times. Islamophobia refers to the unfounded fear, hostility, and discrimination targeted at individuals or communities based on their Muslim faith. This prejudice stems from a variety of sources, including historical events, media portrayals, and geopolitical conflicts.

Acts of terrorism committed by a handful of individuals, who misuse the name of Islam to justify their actions, have unfortunately led to the demonization of an entire faith community. The resulting fear and distrust have reinforced negative stereotypes and deepened the divide between Muslims and non-Muslims.

**The Rise of Extremism**

It is essential to differentiate between mainstream Islam and the radical fringe that perpetrates acts of violence. Extremist ideologies, which claim to adhere to Islam while advocating violence and intolerance, have gained attention in recent years. Such groups exploit socio-political grievances, perpetuating a distorted and politicized version of Islam to recruit followers.

These extremists, however, represent a tiny fraction of the global Muslim population that consists of over 1.8 billion people. Muslim-majority countries themselves have borne the brunt of extremist violence, highlighting the fact that their primary victims are fellow Muslims rather than non-Muslims. It is crucial to remember that just as Christianity or Judaism is not defined by its extremist elements, Islam as a whole should not be judged solely on the actions of a few.

## Addressing Misconceptions

Misconceptions surrounding Islam often stem from a lack of knowledge and understanding. Islam is a religion that preaches peace, justice, and compassion. It emphasizes the importance of charity, benevolence, and community. Yet, misconceptions arise due to cultural differences, misinterpretation of religious texts, or deliberate misinformation.

One common misconception is equating the actions of a few extremists with the entire Muslim population. This generalization fails to account for the vast diversity within the Muslim community, comprising people from various ethnic backgrounds, cultures, and perspectives. Demonizing an entire faith based on the actions of a few is not only unfair but also counterproductive to building understanding and forming meaningful connections.

Another misconception surrounds women's rights in Islam. While some cultural practices might restrict women's freedoms, it is crucial to differentiate between cultural norms and the teachings of Islam. In fact, Islam places great emphasis on the respect, dignity, and rights of women. Prophet Muhammad was an advocate for women's rights, and Islamic history is replete with examples of women holding key roles in society, academia, and politics.

## Promoting Understanding and Tolerance

Addressing Islamophobia, combating extremism, and dispelling misconceptions require a collective effort from individuals, communities, and governments. Education is paramount in fostering understanding and breaking down stereotypes. Encouraging dialogue, learning about different faiths, and engaging with Muslim communities can be constructive steps towards building bridges.

Media outlets also play a crucial role in shaping perceptions of Islam. Balanced and accurate reporting can challenge existing biases and present a more nuanced view of Muslims and their faith. Promoting positive narratives and showcasing the contributions of Muslim individuals and communities to society can help counteract negative stereotypes.

Governments can contribute to this process by implementing policies that promote social inclusion, combat discrimination, and support interfaith dialogue. By fostering an environment that recognizes the value of diversity and encourages mutual respect, governments can lead the way in pushing back against Islamophobia and extremist ideologies.

## Contributions of Muslims to Society & Culture

Through the annals of history, Muslims have made profound and lasting contributions to various realms of human civilization, enriching society and culture in remarkable ways. From the rigorous advancements in scientific inquiry to the breathtaking masterpieces of art and architecture, the impact of Islamic civilization transcends borders and reverberates throughout the ages.

### Advancements in Science and Mathematics

We cannot speak of Muslim contributions to society and culture without acknowledging their pivotal role in advancing the fields of science and mathematics. During the Islamic Golden Age, which spanned the 8th to the 14th century, scholars assimilated, preserved, and expanded upon the knowledge inherited from the Greek, Persian, and Indian civilizations. Muslim scientists made thrilling breakthroughs in various disciplines, including mathematics, optics, medicine, and astronomy.

Pioneers like Al-Farabi, Avicenna, and Al-Khwarizmi made groundbreaking advancements in mathematics. Al-Khwarizmi, often hailed as the "Father of Algebra," introduced the concept of algebra to the world, developing algorithms and describing complex mathematical systems.

Moreover, Muslim astronomers, such as Al-Battani and Nasir al-Din al-Tusi, made significant contributions to understanding celestial movements and furthered the development of astronomical instruments.

## Cultural Legacy in Art and Architecture

Muslims have also left an indelible mark on the world of art and architecture. The splendor of Islamic design is evident in the intricate geometric patterns, delicate calligraphy, and awe-inspiring architecture found in mosques and palaces worldwide. From the iconic Alhambra in Spain to India's Taj Mahal, Islamic architecture epitomizes grandeur, symmetry, and spiritual symbolism.

Calligraphy, the art of beautiful writing, flourished within Islamic culture. Quranic verses and sayings of the Prophet Mohammad were transformed into visually stunning masterpieces, blending text and form in harmonious unity. This unique expression has not only inspired countless artists but has also played a central role in the preservation and dissemination of Islamic literature.

## Literature and Philosophy

The influence of Muslim scholars extended to the realms of literature and philosophy, leaving an indelible mark on the intellectual pursuits of humanity. Renowned philosophers like Al-Kindi, Al-Farabi, and Ibn Sina (Avicenna) played instrumental roles in translating Greek philosophical works into Arabic and expanding upon them. This pivotal effort paved the way for the transmission of Greek philosophy to the Western world.

Muslim scholars were deeply invested in the exploration and debate of various philosophical schools of thought. From theology to ethics, Islamic philosophy embraced critical thinking and rigorous analysis, fostering intellectual debate and contributing to the development of philosophy more broadly.

**Medicine and Healthcare**

Muslims also made significant contributions to the field of medicine, revolutionizing healthcare practices and laying the groundwork for modern medical science. The establishment of the first hospital in Baghdad by Caliph Harun al-Rashid in the 9th century marked a pivotal moment in medical history, where hospitals became centers of scientific inquiry and excellence.

Prominent Muslim physicians such as Ibn Sina and Al-Razi made major advancements in diagnosis, treatment, and pharmacology. Ibn Sina's seminal work, "The Canon of Medicine," became a cornerstone for medical knowledge across Europe and the Islamic world for centuries, showcasing the synthesis of accumulated knowledge and new discoveries.

Muslim contributions to society and culture are far-reaching, spanning across disciplines and continents. From their remarkable advancements in science and mathematics to their architectural and artistic legacies, Muslims have left an indelible mark on the world. Their intellectual curiosity, creativity, and thirst for knowledge continue to inspire generations, serving as a reminder of the immense potential inherent in embracing diverse perspectives.

# Chapter 14

# Conclusion – Embracing Islam

Throughout this book, we have been on a transformative journey, expanding our knowledge and challenging our preconceptions. Through the pages of this book, we have peeled back the layers of misunderstanding, discovering the true essence of Islam and its profound teachings.

Throughout our exploration, we have come to appreciate the diversity within the Islamic faith, understanding that it encompasses a rich tapestry of beliefs, traditions, and interpretations. We have seen how Islam's fundamental principles of peace, justice, and compassion shape the lives of its followers across the globe.

By delving into the historical context and unraveling the intricacies of Islamic practices, we have transcended the stereotypes, biases, and misinformation that often cloud our perception of this noble religion. We have learned that Islam is a faith that teaches respect for all beings, calls for humility and self-reflection, and encourages the pursuit of knowledge and wisdom.

Through its openness and inclusivity, Islam offers a path of spiritual enlightenment and personal growth. It envelops individuals in a global community that values unity, brotherhood, and support. In understanding Islam, we have gained insight into a world that cherishes love, tolerance, and coexistence.

This book has served as a key to unlocking the depths of knowledge and understanding, providing a bridge between cultures and fostering harmony among diverse communities. It reminds us that knowledge is the antidote to ignorance and prejudice, and that by seeking to understand one another, we can create a more peaceful and compassionate world.

## Further Exploration & Learning

Expanding our knowledge about different religions can be a rewarding and enlightening experience. If you have found yourself intrigued by Islam and its rich cultural heritage, you may be interested in delving further into its teachings and exploring its fascinating history. By learning about Islam, we can nurture a greater understanding and appreciation for the beliefs and practices of millions of people around the world.

To embark on this journey, there are several avenues you can pursue. Literature can be an excellent starting point, as it allows for a comprehensive understanding of the Islamic faith. Consider reading the Quran to gain insights into the core beliefs and philosophies of Islam. Additionally, exploring books written by Islamic scholars and historians can provide valuable context and depth to your understanding.

Attending lectures or joining interfaith forums can also be an enriching experience. These platforms often provide the opportunity to engage in open and respectful dialogues with knowledgeable individuals who can shed light on the intricacies of Islamic traditions. By actively participating in these discussions, you can broaden your perspective and challenge any preconceived notions you may have.

Another invaluable way to learn about Islam is through personal connections and interactions with Muslims. Engaging in respectful conversations with members of the Muslim community can offer firsthand insights into their lived experiences, beliefs, and practices. This fosters a sense of empathy and builds bridges of understanding between individuals from different religious backgrounds.

Online resources can be a convenient and easily accessible means of exploring Islam as well. Numerous websites, blogs, and educational platforms dedicated to disseminating accurate information about the Islamic faith can be found. Ensure the sources you choose are reputable and trustworthy, with a focus on providing comprehensive and objective information.

In your pursuit of knowledge, it is essential to approach Islam with an open mind and a commitment to respect and understanding. Recognize that while there may be diverse interpretations and practices within the Islamic faith, it is crucial to approach them with sensitivity and cultural empathy.

Remember, learning about Islam is not just an intellectual exercise but an opportunity to celebrate diversity and forge connections with people of different backgrounds. Ultimately, the purpose of deepening our knowledge about Islam is to promote harmony and foster a world where individuals from all faiths can coexist with mutual respect and understanding.

So, whether you choose to read books, attend lectures, engage in conversations, or explore online resources, embracing the journey of learning about Islam will undoubtedly broaden your horizons and contribute to a more inclusive and tolerant society.

## The Universality & Relevance of Islam in Today's World

In the ever-changing landscape of our global society, where cultures collide and ideologies clash, the universality and relevance of Islam stand as a shining beacon of faith and guidance. With over 1.8 billion followers, Islam is the second-largest religion in the world, encompassing diverse populations across continents. Its teachings and principles lay the foundation for a meaningful and fulfilling life, irrespective of one's cultural background or geographical location.

We've explored that one of the core principles of Islam is the belief in the unity of God, known as Allah. This concept transcends cultural and regional boundaries, resonating with individuals seeking a higher power to worship and find solace in. Whether one is in the bustling streets of Cairo, the serene mountains of Pakistan, or the vibrant cities of Europe and America, the belief in Allah and the teachings of Islam provide a common ground for people to find purpose, comfort, and moral guidance.

The relevance of Islam in today's world cannot be overstated, as it offers solutions to the complex challenges facing humanity. Islam places great emphasis on social justice, urging its followers to treat their fellow human beings with kindness, compassion, and fairness. In an era where inequality, poverty, and prejudice are prevalent, the teachings of Islam offer a blueprint for fostering equality, eradicating discrimination, and nurturing harmony among individuals regardless of their socioeconomic status or perceived differences.

Furthermore, Islam promotes intellectual growth and encourages the pursuit of knowledge. Prophet Muhammad himself once said that "the ink of scholars is more sacred than the blood of martyrs," highlighting the importance of education and the acquisition of knowledge. This emphasis on knowledge resonates in today's technology-driven world, where access to information is at our fingertips. Islam encourages its followers to seek knowledge in various fields, from science and mathematics to humanities and arts, allowing Muslims to contribute meaningfully to the advancement of society in all aspects.

Islam also addresses the existential questions that continue to perplex humanity. Its teachings offer guidance on matters of personal ethics, family values, and societal norms. In an increasingly materialistic world, where moral compasses often waver, Islam provides a steadfast framework for individuals to navigate their lives with integrity, honesty, and humility. The moral and ethical teachings of Islam are as relevant today as they were centuries ago, providing a moral grounding amidst the complexities of the modern world.

The universal nature of Islam is not confined to cultural or ethnic boundaries. It is a faith that transcends race, nationality, and language, creating a sense of unity among its adherents. The annual pilgrimage of Hajj, where millions of Muslims from around the world gather in Mecca, exemplifies this universal bond and showcases the diversity within the global Muslim community. During this sacred journey, individuals not only fulfill one of the five pillars of Islam but also experience a profound sense of togetherness, emphasizing the universality of the faith.

# References

Department of Islamic Art & Authors: Department of Islamic Art. (1 C.E., January 1). *The nature of Islamic art*. The Met's Heilbrunn Timeline of Art History. https://www.metmuseum.org/toah/hd/orna/hd_orna.htm

*Islam: Basic Beliefs*. (n.d.). URI. https://www.uri.org/kids/world-religions/muslim-beliefs

Masjid ar-Rahmah. (2022, February 23). *Beginner's Guide to Understanding Islam - Masjid Ar-Rahmah | Mosque of Mercy*. Masjid ar-Rahmah | Mosque of Mercy. https://www.mymasjid.ca/beginners-guide-understanding-islam/

Rahman, F., Mahdi, M. S., & Schimmel, A. (2024, March 28). *Islam | Religion, Beliefs, Practices, & Facts*. Encyclopedia Britannica. https://www.britannica.com/topic/Islam

Ringgren, H., & Sinai, N. (2024, March 27). *Qur'an | Description, Meaning, History, & Facts*. Encyclopedia Britannica. https://www.britannica.com/topic/Quran

SmallWorld & www.smallworldfs.com. (2024, February 15). A guide to Islamic celebrations and observances. *Small World Money Transfer*. https://www.smallworldfs.com/en/blog/a-guide-to-islamic-celebrations-and-observances

Special, E. S. (2023, July 27). Why do Muslims pray five times a day and what does it signify? *The Economic Times*. https://economictimes.indiatimes.com/news/international/uae/why-do-muslims-pray-five-times-a-day-and-what-does-it-signify/articleshow/94053372.cms?from=mdr

Tech, & Tech. (2023, June 28). *Islam's Moral Code: A Guide to Self-Development*. Facts About the Muslims & the Religion of Islam

Printed in Great Britain
by Amazon